Quotes from **W9-CAE-948**

• • • • • • •

"*The Monogamy Myth* is the best book I have found to help us work through the emotional turmoil of my partner's affair."

"I want to thank you for your book, which I believe has helped the very most in possibly preserving our marriage and our lives."

"I just finished reading your book *The Monogamy Myth*. It was like reading about my own life. All my feelings, thoughts, and actions were on those pages."

"I quickly went out and bought your book . . . I've read and reread it and underlined many pages."

"Your book is truly the best I have ever read on the subject."

"I can't tell you enough about the relief and comfort that your book has brought to me since discovering my husband's affair."

"I would like to thank you for writing your book. My husband and I found it to be the most valuable book we read. Your willingness to share your first-hand experience makes the book most helpful."

"Your book has made such a positive difference. I could identify so easily with your writing and felt so understood and not so alone."

"It was not until I read your book that my pain was finally relieved. I have read your book three times and whenever the pain comes back, I read it again."

"Your book was a Godsend to me, and your realistic view of things was like a soothing balm on my wound."

"I thank you for your painfully honest book and giving me the answers and support I so desperately needed."

"Your book allowed me to release some of the pain in knowing I'm not alone."

"There were times when the words on those pages seemed to help me hang on to little pieces of reality."

ABOUT THE AUTHOR

Peggy Vaughan is an internationally recognized expert in the area of extramarital affairs. Beginning in 1980 with the publication of her personal story in *Beyond Affairs*, Peggy was thrust into a position of responding to the many people across the country who identified with her experience and sought her help. She formed a national support group in the early eighties, and used the learnings from that experience to present a "new understanding" of affairs in *The Monogamy Myth*.

Peggy's "societal perspective" of affairs has catapulted her into the forefront of the growing public discussion of this issue, where she is called upon to comment on the constant stream of news stories related to affairs. But it's her personal commitment to helping people recover from the emotional impact of a partner's affair that has gained her a worldwide following.

The primary arena for her ongoing work with this issue is the Internet, where she maintains an extensive Website (www.vaughan-vaughan.com) and coordinates two separate support groups for BAN (Beyond Affairs Network). She also serves as the Expert on Affairs for the Online Psych area of AOL (America Online), responding to questions about extramarital affairs that are sent to "Ask Peggy."

Peggy has been married for over forty years, has two grown children and two grandchildren and makes her home in La Jolla, California.

In addition to *The Monogamy Myth*, Peggy has written *Beyond Affairs, Making Love Stay,* and *Life Design Workbook,* all co-authored with her husband James.

THE
MONOGAMY
MYTH

• • • • • • •

A Personal Handbook for
Recovering from Affairs

• • • • • • •

PEGGY VAUGHAN

NEWMARKET PRESS
New York

10 9 8 7 6

Library of Congress Cataloging-in-Publication Data
Vaughan, Peggy.
The monogamy myth : a personal handbook for
recovering from affairs / Peggy Vaughan.
p. cm.
Updated and rev. ed. of: The monogamy myth : a new
understanding of affairs and how to survive them, 1989.
Includes bibliographical references.
ISBN 1-55704-362-0. — ISBN 1-55704-353-1 (pbk.)
1. Adultery—United States—Psychological aspects.
2. Communication in marriage—United States. I. Title.
HQ806.V38 1998
306.73'6—dc21   98-5029
                                                CIP

Quantity Purchases
Companies, professional groups, clubs, and other organizations may
qualify for special terms when ordering quantities of this title. For
information, write Special Sales, Newmarket Press, 18 East 48th Street,
New York, NY 10017, Tel. (212) 832-3575; Fax: (212) 832-3629;
E-mail: mailbox@newmarketpress.com

www.newmarketpress.com

Book design by MaryJane DiMassi

Manufactured in the United States of America

For information regarding seminars or speaking engagements,
contact Peggy Vaughan, P.O. Box 1942, La Jolla, California 92038.
You may also visit her Website (www.vaughan-vaughan.com)
for information about seminars or speeches as well as
for information about joining BAN (Beyond Affairs Network).

CONTENTS

• • • • • • •

ACKNOWLEDGMENTS

• • • • • • •

When you expose as much of yourself in your writing as I do, it's essential to have a strong base of support and encouragement. I'm very grateful for the richness of my personal support system, and I want to publicly express my appreciation to these very special people.

First, to James, my lifelong partner in love and in work, for his constant support for what I have to say and his confidence in my ability to say it. And to the other special people in my life: my son, Andy; my daughter and son-in-law, Vicki and Dan; and my two wonderful granddaughters for the joy of being part of their lives.

I also want to thank those people who have contributed directly to the production of this book. To my agent and friend, Laurie Harper, for her belief in the importance of this work and her personal dedication to its success. To my editor, Theresa Burns, whose keen organizational skills brought essential structure and clarity to the manuscript. And to Keith Hollaman for his significant contribution in handling the editorial details during the final stages of producing the book.

To Esther Margolis and the entire staff of Newmarket Press, who provided the kind of professional expertise and personal support that is the dream of every author. And to Jeff Mariotte, my friend and bookseller, for keeping me up to date on happenings in the book world.

Finally, to the members of BAN (Beyond Affairs Network), with love and appreciation for sharing their lives with me—and providing the inspiration for this book.

A Personal Note from the Author

• • • • • • •

Dear Reader,

There have been some significant changes related to the issue of affairs since *The Monogamy Myth* was first published almost a decade ago.

- There's more public exposure of people having affairs.
- More married women are having affairs and more husbands are reaching out for help.
- The Internet is exploding with opportunities for developing Online Affairs.
- There are more resources (like my own Website) for helping people recover from affairs.
- There's a constantly growing focus on this issue by the media.
- People are becoming more aware of the prevalence and the importance of this issue.

There is now an openness to the ideas and the help offered in *The Monogamy Myth* that simply didn't exist when it was originally published. However, despite the increased attention to this problem, I have NOT seen a change in the degree of pain and devastation experienced by the person whose partner has an affair. The myths reinforcing the idea that affairs happen only because of personal failure have made it extremely difficult for people to recover their self-esteem and rebuild their relationships. So the message of *The Monogamy Myth* is still desperately needed, both by those personally facing this issue in their own lives—and by society as a whole.

Much of the increased openness to discussing affairs is due to the growing public exposure of this behavior. For instance, there was a wall of silence (until after their deaths) about the affairs of some past presidents of the United States—most notably President Roosevelt's long-term affair and President Kennedy's multiple affairs. In contrast, there is detailed public exposure and an almost insatiable public discussion of this issue regarding President Clinton. And it's hard to pick up a paper or turn on the TV without being confronted with glaring headlines of the latest scandal or exposé.

While this exposure serves to break through some of the secrecy of the past, there's still an enormous amount of hypocrisy involved. We still act as if the people who are at the center of the stories (whether in the military, the government, or the private sector) are somehow different or unique—when, in fact, they are simply the ones who get *caught* and are put in the position of either "lying" or receiving "punishment." Their uniqueness is not in their behavior; it's in the fact that their behavior is *exposed*. This is not an excuse for their behavior, but it's an important perspective if we are to overcome our hypocrisy and acknowledge the prevalence of affairs as the first steps to addressing this problem in a responsible way.

In fact, we see growing numbers of "regular people" coming forward to tell their story. Back in 1980, James and I were the first couple to appear on a daytime talk show discussing their personal experience in dealing with extramarital affairs and staying together as a couple. It was very responsibly handled and was a positive experience. But through the years, talk shows have contributed to both the best and the worst aspects of dealing with affairs. They have promoted the idea of talking more openly about this issue—but they have increasingly done so in an irresponsible way. It's my hope that we can continue to deal more openly with the issue of affairs while protecting and respecting the feelings of those who struggle personally with this experience.

While much of the media attention is based on appealing to the sensationalistic aspects of this problem, more and more often it is being treated with the importance it deserves. For instance, I was pleased to be involved in a newsmagazine show that did an entire hour on affairs, focusing less on the typical titillation and voyeurism and more on providing a glimpse into the human toll of our general failure to deal responsibly with this issue.

So while we might once have dismissed the story of an affair as being irrelevant to our lives, we're beginning to pay more attention now that those who are publicly accused of having affairs include people from all walks of life: the military, clergy, high-ranking politicians—even royalty. Despite the growing numbers of affairs that are exposed in this way, we still tend to think (hope?) this problem is limited only to certain kinds of people in bad marriages. This thinking is seriously challenged when exposures include people we believe to have exemplary marriages, like Frank Gifford or Bill Cosby.

While every individual is responsible for their own actions (and the consequences of those actions), it's a mistake to think that only people with personal weaknesses have affairs. It's far more complicated than that. As I explain in *The Monogamy Myth*, the prevalence of affairs makes this more than just a personal problem; it's a societal problem as well.

I know firsthand the pain that comes from viewing affairs strictly as a personal failure. I suffered silently for seven years while suspecting my husband's affairs—because I was too embarrassed to tell anyone. My own personal struggle is what sustains my effort to help those who continue to suffer in silence because of that false belief. When a person is privately dealing with the emotional impact of a partner's affair, they can dramatically increase their chances of recovery by understanding the prevalence of affairs, the societal factors that contribute to them—and ultimately the fact that it's more than just personal failure.

When I learned this lesson myself, it allowed me to go from feeling like a victim ("Why me?") to realizing that it wasn't just me; this could have happened to anyone. I also found this thinking helpful the next time I faced a serious life crisis. Three years after *The Monogamy Myth* was first published, I developed breast cancer—and I was able to draw on my earlier experience in several ways: first, I felt no need to keep it secret, and being able to openly discuss it allowed me to gain invaluable information and support. And second, I didn't have the inclination to say, Why me? I had learned the lesson that many life problems we tend to think are personal (and possibly our fault) are in fact more a reflection of their prevalence in society as a whole.

One of the changes in my life that developed as a result of my experience in dealing with affairs was one that was quite unexpected. An early reviewer of *The Monogamy Myth*, who gave the book a very positive review, added this personal comment: "When some women's husbands have affairs, they get a divorce. Others stay married, but suffer in silence. Peggy Vaughan's husband had affairs—and she made a career out of it!"

While I would never have chosen to go through this experience, I proudly accept that description of what happened as a result. I have, in fact, devoted almost all my time to helping people deal with the issue of affairs since I went public with my own story in 1980. Through the years I have learned an enormous amount from the people who have shared their experiences with me. In the early eighties I formed a support group called BAN (Beyond Affairs Network), and it was due to what I learned from those early BAN members that I developed the perspective I share in this book.

I am now in the midst of another steep learning curve based on my current window on the world—my Website on the Internet. On the Website, I now have a new and improved version of BAN with members from forty-seven states and ten other countries. They openly and candidly share their innermost feelings about their efforts to cope with a partner's affair. During the first six months of this new BAN, I read fifteen thousand messages posted on the Message Board by people struggling with this issue. It's been gratifying to see that everything I originally wrote in *The Monogamy Myth* is right on target. Of the thousands of questions I've been asked about dealing with affairs, I rarely hear a question that I haven't already addressed in the book.

One development related to affairs (which many people still tend to ignore) is that this has become an "equal opportunity" problem in that both men and women regularly face this devastating experience. In fact, 40 percent of the current BAN members are men. And one of the most striking aspects of BAN is that there is virtually NO difference between men and women in their efforts to cope with a partner's affair—or in their ability to be supportive of others in similar circumstances. When reading the BAN Message Board without noting the sex of the person making any particular comment, it is virtually impossible to determine whether it came from a man or a woman. Unfortunately, there has been very little support available to help men in working on these issues; but since *The Monogamy Myth* is not slanted toward one sex or the other, it is a resource for all alike.

Of course, the increase in men dealing with their wives' affairs highlights the fact that there has been a continuing increase in married women having affairs. Some factors that may have contributed to this include: having increased opportunities (through work or through contacts on the Internet), being more willing to risk divorce (due to financial independence), or less willing to conform to traditional expectations of the role of "wife." Also, the societal "message" to women reflects a more accepting attitude toward women's affairs—as illustrated by the generally positive light in which they are depicted in books and movies, most notably *The Bridges of Madison County*. This attitude is also reflected in the material used to promote several nonfiction books on the subject and in the words of encouragement used to promote one popular novel about affairs: "Every woman should have at least one in her lifetime."

Another major change related to this issue is the tremendous rise in what has become known as Online Affairs—affairs that begin (and supposedly will remain) on the Internet. The growing popularity of this medium for affairs might be thought to be an effort to avoid AIDS or other risks associated with physical contact. But there has been no discernable decline in affairs due to AIDS or to any other factor. People having affairs tend to rationalize their behavior, and a part of that rationalization is ignoring or denying the possibility of any negative consequences.

I have had a front-row seat to the specific process of rationalization associated with having Online Affairs by virtue of serving as the Expert on Affairs for the Online Psych area of AOL (America Online). In my first six months as "Ask Peggy," I received more than one thousand letters—and, not surprisingly, a large percentage of the letters dealt with the issue of Online Affairs. I have added some detailed information about Online Affairs to the last chapter of the book under the section on Preventing Affairs. Like other issues related to affairs, this should be of interest and concern to everyone—whether or not you are currently on the Internet.

The bottom line is that few people will avoid being personally touched by an affair. If not in your own relationship, you will almost certainly be affected through the experience of a friend or family member. (Among the current members of BAN, 77 percent have told a friend about their partner's affair and 62 percent have told a family member.) Since you're unlikely to avoid this issue, you are wise to be prepared in advance by having as much understanding as possible. It's very difficult to think clearly if you wait until you're in the midst of trying to deal it.

The Monogamy Myth is an invaluable life preserver for the person who is already facing this problem and needs help in dealing with the emotional impact. This book is, as the subtitle suggests, a personal handbook for recovering from affairs. It is also a unique resource for anyone who genuinely wants to understand the public's role and responsibility in addressing this issue.

I encourage you to read this book and to discuss it with others. The more responsible, open discussion we can have about affairs, the less pain there will be for everyone concerned. For ongoing support in your effort to deal with all important life issues, especially the life-altering issue of affairs, I hope you will visit my Website at http://www.vaughan-vaughan.com.

Peggy Vaughan,
January 1998

THE MONOGAMY MYTH

· · · · · · ·

Author's note: In keeping with accepted guidelines for nonsexist writing, extensive use of the pronoun *they* (especially the possessive form *their*) has been made when referring to a singular noun.

Introduction: The Myth and the Reality

Most of us expect monogamy to be a normal part of marriage (or any committed relationship). This was certainly my assumption when I married my childhood sweetheart at age nineteen. I grew up with no firsthand knowledge of affairs and no idea that it was a subject of any concern to me. I simply took it for granted that my marriage would be monogamous.

My expectations of monogamy were shattered after eleven years of marriage. It was at that point that my husband, James, started having affairs. When I first began to suspect it, I couldn't bring myself to believe this could happen. He was a preministerial college student when we married, and we shared the same traditional values of marriage and monogamy. But there were many changes in our lives during those first years of marriage. He decided to become a psychologist, and later a professor, and I moved into a more traditional role as wife and mother. It was during this period that he began having affairs.

James's affairs continued for seven years, and during that time my suspicions grew stronger and stronger. But I found myself incapable of confronting him. If it were true, I felt I'd have to get a divorce to save my pride. And I felt anxious and uncertain about my ability to make it on my own with two small children. So instead of confronting him, I began working on myself, trying to gain strength and confidence in my ability to deal with whatever might happen.

The real breakthrough came when he left the university setting and we began working together as psychological consultants to corporations and other organizations. A major part of this work involved our conducting workshops and seminars on communication, trust, and life/work planning. James became uncomfortable with the idea of working together on issues of honesty and trust while being dishonest with me about something so important to our relationship. Eventually, he volunteered the information I had wondered about for so long, admitting that he had had a series of affairs.

Fortunately, by the time he told me about his affairs, I had grown strong enough to face the situation and see if we could work through it. By continuing to talk about everything related to the affairs and our feelings during that time, we were able to develop an honest, monogamous marriage again.

We gradually began using our experience in dealing with affairs in the workshops we were conducting to illustrate how honest communication can allow people to work through problems and differences, regardless of how difficult or seemingly insurmountable. The positive reactions to what we had to say gradually led us to begin writing a book about our experience, a process that took six years. However, we didn't anticipate the difficulty we encountered in getting it published. We finally resorted to self-publishing the book, putting a second mortgage on our home to finance the project. It was 1980 when *Beyond Affairs* finally came out. Despite our belief in what we were doing, we were unprepared for the reactions we received. The response completely changed my life.

I didn't realize at the time just how unusual it was for a couple to talk personally about their own experience with affairs, but the reaction from the media was overwhelming. We appeared on about a hundred television and radio talk shows, from "Donahue" to "To Tell the Truth," to publicize the book. This allowed us to reach a large number of people, and our openness brought a wide range of reactions—from business associates, family, friends, and the general public.

The most unexpected (and unpleasant) reaction was from some business associates. As independent consultants, we'd been working with a large corporation for several years at the time the book was published. The top people at the company knew about James's affairs and knew that I knew about them (since we had used examples from this experience in helping companies deal more effectively with interpersonal issues). They even knew in advance that we were writing the book, and they assured us it made no difference to our work with them.

However, following our appearance on the "Today" program, we were told that our contract would not be renewed. They acknowledged that our public discussion of the subject of affairs was the reason. So even though we were professionals who were sharing our experience as a way of bringing more understanding to this problem, they couldn't accept the idea that we had "gone public."

Within my own family, there were a variety of reactions, both to the knowledge of the affairs themselves and to the fact that we publicly discussed them. I had told my mother the whole story several years before the publication of the book, so she was not shocked by the revelations it contained. But, understandably, she was not thrilled with the idea of my talking publicly about something she considered so personal. She acknowledged, however, that she thought the book would be a significant benefit to others; she just wished someone other than her daughter had written it.

Our kids were not a problem for us, but they were a problem for a lot of other people. I don't believe there was a single talk show where someone (either the host or a member of the audience) didn't ask, rather incredulously, what our children thought of the book, or of our telling our story. Our kids were sixteen and eighteen at the time, but they had known about our situation for five years and were well aware of our work with this issue during that time, both personally and professionally. So our public discussion of the experience wasn't strange or troublesome to them. Their only problem was wondering why everyone *thought* they should have a problem.

We found that our close friends became even closer and our social acquaintances became more distant following the publicity around the book. I guess this shouldn't have been surprising, but it was something we simply hadn't considered in advance.

The most gratifying of all the reactions were the ones from the general public. We had anticipated some criticism based on people misunderstanding our motives or simply disagreeing with the idea of speaking publicly about our experience in dealing with affairs. To our surprise, we received very little criticism; and when it came, it was invariably from someone who only saw us on media appearances and had not read the book.

We wrote *Beyond Affairs* because we genuinely believed that what we had to say would be helpful to others, and the overall response bore that out. A clergyman in Seattle, who operated a counseling center, told us he was using our book in his group sessions with couples dealing with the issue of affairs. A sociologist in New Jersey began using the book in courses on marriage and the family. We heard from other professionals as well, but the most significant reaction came from those people struggling with affairs themselves. By the time the mass market edition of the book came out the following year, we'd received hundreds of letters and phone calls from people who identified with our story.

While many of the letters were from women who felt I had perfectly expressed their feelings, I also heard from men who had dealt with their wives' affairs, from couples in which both partners had had affairs, from unmarried couples who were struggling with monogamy, and from a few same-sex couples who were dealing with the pain that affairs can bring. I was extremely moved by the outpouring of feelings that came from these people who were strangers, but who were talking like close friends.

I wanted to support their efforts to survive their experience with affairs, so I responded personally to every letter. I also received many phone calls late at night. It was painful to hear the sense of desperation and isolation expressed by most of the people who called. I felt inadequate to do much in a one-time response, whether by mail or by phone, and always invited them to write or call again.

This was the beginning of my personal dedication to helping others in dealing with the experience of affairs. But I could see I wouldn't be able to keep up with all the contacts on an individual basis. If I were to continue, I had to bring some organization to the effort. So I asked those who would like to maintain the contact to fill out a sheet providing some basic information: how long they'd been married, how long since the affair, how much it had been discussed, whether they had sought counseling, and whether or not they were still married.

I asked them to agree to have their names and addresses put on a list that would be distributed only to others in the same situation. This formed the basis of a support network ("Beyond Affairs Network" or BAN) where they could contact each other, as well as make it possible for me to put people in touch who might be especially helpful to each other. Since they were scattered all over the country, as well as Canada, there were only a few locations with enough people to hold face-to-face meetings. Otherwise, all the contact was by mail. Even this kind of contact was difficult for some people, since they felt they had to keep the information hidden from their mates. Those who knew their spouse didn't want them to discuss their personal life with anyone else arranged to have friends or family members receive their BAN mail, and several even rented special post office boxes just for this correspondence.

I began to write a monthly newsletter about affairs, using their letters to me to determine the most common issues to be addressed. I wrote the newsletter every month for the next three years, but I also continued to write personal letters, developing a deep friendship with many of the people. Through the years, either due to my own travel or because of trips they made to my area of the country, I met with about twenty of the BAN members in person. After all these years, I'm still in touch with several members of this original group, and they continue to provide a source of insight and perspective.

The overwhelming message I've gotten from this group through the years is that dealing with extramarital affairs is a life-altering experience. Their quotes and case histories used throughout this book illustrate its devastating impact. Some of them had been married only two years at the time an affair was discovered; others had been married as long as thirty-nine years. Regardless of when or how it happened in the marriage, it became an issue that rocked the relationship to its core and constituted a dramatic change in their lives. Here's the way one person described its effect:

When a person witnesses a murder, they describe how they relive it, and how the shock is still with them and has changed their whole perception of the world. This is so easily accepted by people; yet dealing with the trauma of an affair is not—though it too dramatically changes life, and your perception of it, forever.

The reason dealing with an affair is such a devastating experience with such long-lasting effects is that our beliefs about monogamy have led us to expect that we won't have to face the issue of affairs—and to feel like a personal failure if it happens. This way of thinking is based on what I have come to call the Monogamy Myth.

THE MONOGAMY MYTH
· · · · · · ·

The Monogamy Myth is the belief that monogamy is the norm in our society and that it is supported by society as a whole. The effect of believing that most marriages or committed relationships are monogamous is that if an affair happens, it's seen strictly as a personal failure of the people involved. This leads to personal blame, personal shame, wounded pride, and almost universal feelings of devastation.

The reality is that monogamy is *not* the norm, not by today's standards, anyway. *Conservative* estimates are that 60 percent of men and 40 percent of women will have an extramarital affair. These figures are even more significant when we consider the total number of marriages involved, since it's unlikely that all the men and women having affairs happen to be married to each other. If even half of the women having affairs (or 20 percent) are married to men *not* included in the 60 percent having affairs, then at least one partner will have an affair in approximately 80 percent of all marriages. With this many marriages affected, it's unreasonable to think affairs are due *only* to the failures and shortcomings of individual husbands or wives.

According to the Monogamy Myth, society as a whole is supportive of monogamy and of people's efforts to remain monogamous, leading people to expect to have a monogamous marriage.

This reinforces the idea of personal failure for those people who fail to achieve monogamy.

In reality, while society gives lip service to monogamy, there are significant societal factors that actually support and encourage affairs. This is not to say that all the blame should be placed on society. That would be just as shortsighted as blaming only the particular people involved. But we can make a significant difference, both in the incidence of affairs and in the difficulty of dealing with them, by taking a broader look at the social structure within which they take place.

Seeing problems in a societal context is already happening in a number of other areas. We're coming to see the underlying conditions that lead to violence instead of focusing only on individual acts of violence. We're coming to see the lifestyle habits that lead to disease instead of focusing only on individual incidences of illness. In the same way, we need to see the factors in society that contribute to affairs instead of focusing only on the individual who has an affair.

We need to reject the Monogamy Myth, not to excuse those who have affairs, but to relieve the sense of shame and inadequacy felt by their mates. Since they keep their shame and anger hidden, they seldom get enough perspective to completely recover from these feelings, regardless of whether they stay married or get a divorce. Surviving this experience if it has happened (or avoiding it if it hasn't) is best accomplished by dealing with reality, not holding on to a myth.

NEW HOPE FOR MONOGAMY
• • • • • • •

When I discovered my husband's affairs, I had a hard time coping with the idea that our marriage was not monogamous in the way I had assumed it would be. While I gave up my belief in the Monogamy Myth, I didn't give up my hope for monogamy. I still believe in monogamy and think it's attainable. But achieving monogamy calls for making some drastic changes in our thinking. The irony of the Monogamy Myth is that it keeps us from dealing with the issues that need to be addressed in order to make monogamy a more attainable goal.

The best hope for monogamy lies in rejecting the idea that a couple can *assume* monogamy without discussing the issue, or that they can *assure* monogamy by making threats as to what they would do if it happened. Either of these paths creates a cycle of dishonesty. In either case, people don't feel free to admit being attracted to someone else. If they don't admit these attractions, then they won't admit being tempted. And if they don't admit being tempted, then they certainly won't admit it if and when they finally act on the attraction. The effect on the relationship is to cause it to be filled with jealousy and suspicion, as well as making it *less* likely that it will be monogamous.

The hope for monogamy lies in making a conscious choice that specifically involves a commitment to honesty. In making this choice, both partners realize that attractions to others are likely, indeed inevitable, no matter how much they love each other. So they engage in ongoing honest communication about the reality of the temptations and how to avoid the consequences of acting on those temptations. The effect on the relationship is to create a sense of closeness and a knowledge of each other that replaces suspicion with trust, making it *more* likely that it will be monogamous.

Monogamy is something most people say they believe in and want for themselves. Every survey ever done on this question shows a high percentage of people think monogamy is important to marriage and that affairs are wrong. But a belief in monogamy as an ideal doesn't prevent large numbers of people from having extramarital affairs. We need to make a commitment to face the reality of affairs and address the issue in a more responsible way, both individually and as a society.

This means challenging many of our most cherished beliefs about monogamy and affairs. It will be hard to question some of our old assumptions—and even harder to give them up. Our attitudes about monogamy and affairs are so ingrained that we find it difficult to consider anything that deviates from those beliefs. But it's essential if we're to gain understanding and perspective about this very emotional issue.

A new understanding of affairs involves more than just changing our thinking about the cause of affairs. It also includes changing our thinking about how to handle the issues of blame, secrecy, self-esteem, getting help, and whether or not to stay in the marriage. The following chapters will examine each of these aspects, reviewing the old ways of thinking and presenting a new understanding of each issue as it relates to the overall understanding of affairs. This will include concrete ideas for couples who want to stay in the marriage and work through their personal experience with affairs. It also will include suggestions for achieving personal survival, regardless of whether the marriage survives. Self-help strategies alone seldom bring full recovery from this experience, either as a couple or individually. Recovery depends on getting beyond our strictly personal view of affairs to an understanding of them within a broader framework.

WHY IT'S EVERYBODY'S BUSINESS
• • • • • •

One reason affairs are everybody's business (regardless of whether or not they are directly involved) is because *all* of us are responsible for the factors in society that contribute to them. These societal factors will be discussed in chapter 2, and the final chapter contains suggestions about how to work toward diminishing this societal support for affairs.

Another reason for gaining a greater understanding of monogamy and affairs is to make things better for our children and the generations to follow. We need to question what we're teaching our young people about honesty as long as we perpetuate a belief in the Monogamy Myth.

The most immediate reason we need to be informed about affairs is because no one is immune from having affairs disrupt their lives or the lives of those they care about; affairs happen to all kinds of people, in all walks of life. Traditionally our attitude has been that unless it touches us personally, we deal with it by ignoring it, denying it, or condemning it. Unfortunately, this does nothing either to help deter affairs or to deal with their consequences. If we're to be the kind of caring, compassionate society we aspire to be, we can't turn our backs on the countless people who are suffering alone.

While much of the focus of dealing with affairs is on couples who are married, unmarried couples struggle with many of the same issues of trust and commitment. The problems created by affairs and the reactions of the people involved readily apply to any couple in a committed relationship, so the ideas about monogamy and affairs discussed in this book are relevant for all couples, regardless of their marital status.

The assumptions about monogamy supported by the Monogamy Myth have made it extremely difficult for most couples in a committed relationship to openly discuss the subjects of monogamy, sexual attraction to others, and outside affairs. But I've seen in my own life what a difference it can make when you're willing to face these issues realistically. I'm not saying it's easy, because there were times when I didn't think we would make it.

But I do know one thing: the day my husband told me about his affairs has become very important for us, in many ways more important than our wedding anniversary. While it was a day that turned my world upside down, it's one that we still celebrate today, after all these years. It's not the day itself we're celebrating; rather, it was the honesty that began that day. It resulted in our making a commitment to be honest about all important issues affecting our relationship. When I think how far we've come, I know there's hope for others in gaining a new understanding of affairs—and surviving them.

PART I

WHY AFFAIRS HAPPEN

1
· · · · · · ·

Beyond Personal Blame

The first question most people ask when they learn of their mate's affair is, "Why?" And the answers they come up with are usually based on personal blame. They blame themselves, their partner, their relationship, or the third party. This reaction is predictable in light of the fact that the Monogamy Myth leads to seeing affairs only as a personal problem, a personal failure of the people involved. By examining the effects of this personal view of affairs, we can better understand just how destructive this approach can be to the efforts of people to understand and deal with their experience.

BLAMING YOURSELF
· · · · · · ·

I'm still trying to cope with the reasons for his affairs: too fat, too skinny, too much sex, too little sex, too neat, too sloppy—and the list goes on and on.

I can't help but feel inadequate. My thoughts are, 'What's wrong with me?' Was I not successful enough to suit her? What was she looking for that I didn't provide?

When people look for reasons to explain why their partner has an affair, they inevitably start with themselves. Every weakness they ever worried about becomes a source of concern. They look for some personal inadequacy (either real or imagined) that might have caused the affair. Unfortunately, this way of thinking has been reinforced by most of the popular books, articles, and advice columns about how to prevent affairs.

One of the most common conclusions by a person who feels personally responsible for their partner's affair is, "I wasn't sexy enough." There's a standard line of thinking that if someone gets the sex they want at home, they won't look for it somewhere else. This assumes that the only reason people have affairs is because there's something sexually lacking at home. But since sex is not the only reason for having an affair, good sex certainly can't prevent it. In fact, many people report the outside sex much less satisfying than the sex at home. Usually, the desire is for newness and variety, and has little to do with the degree of satisfaction with the primary partner.

Another common source of personal blame is thinking, "I wasn't attentive enough to my partner's needs and desires." This thinking is based on the belief that constantly boosting a partner's ego can keep them from looking for someone else who will. While genuinely paying attention to your partner is positive, catering to their every wish (as a ploy to keep them from having an affair) is usually transparent and contributes to a lack of respect for your feelings or your right to honesty, fairness, and equality.

The personal blaming often expands to include any area in which a person thinks they failed to be "the best." They see their partner's affair as a sign that they weren't smart enough, or successful enough, or attractive enough, or interesting enough. In fact, there's no way to "beat out" the competition in every area of life. Focusing on being the best in one area diminishes the amount of time and energy available for succeeding in others. Since nobody's perfect, it's easy to find some personal shortcoming to blame as the cause of a partner's affair.

For instance, a woman who was a full-time homemaker and mother was convinced that if only she'd been out in the world, she would have been a more interesting partner and her husband wouldn't have had an affair. At the same time, another woman who was career-oriented was convinced that her involvement with her career limited her time and attention to her husband and was the reason he had an affair.

Accepting personal responsibility for determining the behavior of another person inevitably leads to failure. My experience is a good example of the false premise of this kind of thinking. I tried to do everything possible to keep my husband "interested." I was always dieting (even though I wasn't overweight). I kept myself "fixed" with makeup, I wore sexy underwear, I was sexually active in bed and always available and eager. I was the consummate mother, the gourmet cook, the gracious hostess for parties and dinners for his business colleagues, and the lively and well-liked social partner. I was active in current political causes, but I also took care of everything that might make his life easier, including doing all the packing for his frequent business trips, paying the bills and handling all our financial matters (including our tax returns), and generally doing any and everything I could think of to be such an ideal wife that he wouldn't consider having an affair.

Later, when James reflected on his reaction to my efforts during that time, he recalled thinking, "Wow, this is great. I've got this terrific wife who's doing all these wonderful things—and I've got my affairs too!" He felt like the luckiest man in the world.

It's unreasonable for anyone to think they can prevent their partner from having an affair, or to think they're personally to blame if it happens. But some people have an overwhelming sense of personal failure when they learn of their mate's affair. One woman, who felt her husband's affair symbolized her failure as a wife, took an overdose of sleeping pills. By the time she was discovered, the doctors were barely able to save her with emergency surgery. Her immediate reaction when she regained consciousness was that she had failed again; she couldn't even succeed at taking her own life.

With time, she came to see her suicide attempt as an impulsive act of desperation based on a misguided sense of blame. She felt very fortunate to have survived, and gradually gained an appreciation of herself as a person who deserved to live and to enjoy life. It's not unusual for such a disastrous event to open a person's eyes to a more realistic perspective of whatever difficulty they face. But hopefully people can learn to overcome the tendency to blame themselves for their partner's affair prior to any such trauma.

Of course, even when people succeed in avoiding the inclination to blame themselves, they still feel a tremendous need to figure out who or what is to blame for their mate's affair.

BLAMING YOUR PARTNER
• • • • • • •

Up until that time I had great respect for my wife. But she's not the person I thought she was. Now I find that I doubt everything about her and I really don't know if I love her.

He doesn't deserve someone like me. He's exposed himself as a thoughtless, cruel, and uncaring person.

Those people who avoid blaming themselves for their partner's affair are likely to think, "Since it's not *my* fault, then it must be my partner's fault." They may see their partner as totally to blame and feel overcome with anger. The intensity of these feelings gets expressed in a variety of ways, often in seemingly bizarre behavior. One man went into such a rage upon learning of his wife's affair that he went into her closet and cut up every piece of clothing she owned.

This man's behavior was not as strange as it might at first seem, since he had been feeling uneasy about his wife's growing wardrobe of new clothes and the fact that she had been looking entirely *too* good to suit his feelings of jealousy. When he discovered her affair, he immediately made the connection between the affair and her new clothes, venting his anger on them as a symbol of the rage he felt about the affair.

Even if people avoid such a violent reaction when learning of a mate's affair, those who place all the blame on their partner usually become extremely critical of every possible weakness their partner may have. The list can be endless, but it usually focuses on judgments about character: Their partner is not mature enough, has weak moral principles, or is not secure enough as a man or a woman.

The person whose partner has an affair is likely to be very bitter and resentful toward their partner for their feelings of embarrassment and pain. And these feelings are usually reinforced by those with whom they share this information. One man told of reluctantly confiding in his best friend, who told him he was crazy for even listening to anything his wife had to say in her own defense. The friend said her actions had spoken for her; that nothing she could say would change the fact that she was a selfish, castrating bitch.

This is not an unusual reaction, since there's a great deal of support in society for placing the entire blame on the person who succumbed to having an affair, regardless of the situation. Our tendency is to judge them quite harshly, seeing them as evil or "sick" and in need of help to determine what caused them to do such a thing. We wonder why they bothered to get married if they didn't mean to be faithful, and we want to see them punished for what they did. We are self-righteous in our attitude because we're convinced they are deviant or immoral people. But in most instances, they're not bad people and don't deserve to be unilaterally blamed for what happened. While each of us is ultimately responsible for our behavior, the decision to have an affair doesn't take place in isolation; it is influenced by many other factors in society (which will be discussed in the following chapter).

BLAMING THE RELATIONSHIP
· · · · · · ·

We were never right for each other from the beginning. I thought she would change, but the relationship never really had a chance to work. We were just too different in our backgrounds and interests.

I know we got married too young. Everyone said we should wait, and they were right. This wouldn't have happened if we'd had more sexual experience before marriage.

The next most obvious place to look for problems causing an affair is the relationship itself. Everything comes under scrutiny. One of the most popular areas of blame is the idea of marrying too young and not sowing enough wild oats prior to marriage, thus leading to affairs later on. This, like a lot of things, *can* be a contributing factor. But it certainly doesn't explain the many people who sow their wild oats before marriage and then find in a couple of years that they miss what they gave up. And while most people start out marriage planning to give up outside sex, some never even slow down. I know of several instances where people had sex with others in the wedding party just prior to the wedding. Another typical relationship problem that gets blamed as the cause of an affair is lack of communication. It's difficult to see how this can be judged as the explanation for an affair, since poor communication is seldom the problem in and of itself; it's often a symptom of other problems.

But since there are problems in every relationship, there's always something that can be identified as lacking. To assume a cause and effect between the particular problem and having affairs is much too narrow an explanation of such a complicated issue. No matter which factors are identified in a particular relationship, there are any number of other factors that could just as easily have been blamed for an affair. The bottom line is that we can't fully understand why a particular person has an affair just by analyzing their marriage.

BLAMING THE THIRD PARTY

• • • • • • •

As far as I am concerned, the type of woman that will have affairs with married men is a disgrace to womanhood.

He took advantage of her by impressing her with his money and power. I don't know how she couldn't see him for what he was—a self-centered bastard who thought he was "God's gift to women."

Whenever someone wants to avoid blaming themselves, their partner, or their relationship for an affair, the third party provides a very tempting target. Much of the anger at the spouse who had an affair gets directed at the third party, especially if there's a decision to stay married. Some people feel that transferring some of the intensity of their feelings to the third party makes it easier to deal with rebuilding the relationship. One woman reported arriving at the conclusion that it was completely the fault of the other woman, that if it weren't for her, there wouldn't have been an affair at all. But it's much more likely that an affair results from the overall situation, not from any seduction by a particular person.

Opportunity and circumstances play a far more important role in determining an affair than any specific qualities of the third party. This is why there are so many affairs among people who work together or have other opportunities for developing close relationships. Of course, the third party gets very little understanding from anyone in this situation, including society as a whole. There's a tendency to see them as a kind of ogre. We'll focus on getting a clearer perspective of the third party in a later chapter dealing specifically with their role in extramarital affairs.

WHY WE TAKE IT PERSONALLY
· · · · · · ·

While the primary reason for this personal view of affairs is our belief in the Monogamy Myth, there are other significant factors that reinforce this view. In studying this issue for the past fifteen years and exploring related issues in the course of conducting workshops and seminars on values, perception, and cultural norms, I found a number of forces contributing to this personal view of affairs.

THE ADVICE OF EXPERTS

Since many people look to the opinion of experts as validation of the correctness of their opinions, the professional posture regarding the reasons for affairs has a powerful impact on others in society. Not only has the personal view of affairs been the assumption of the general population, but most experts agree. In fact, the standard advice of counselors, therapists, and advice columnists has been for couples to examine themselves and the conditions within their relationship to determine why an affair happened.

Since most people in the helping professions have their training or orientation in terms of psychology rather than sociology, they tend to see things in terms of personal, individual problems. They bring this bias to their work with couples dealing with affairs, and this personal orientation reinforces the attitude that affairs are due exclusively to individual weaknesses. This approach is considered to be the appropriate one when couples are in counseling, as illustrated by the following description of the role of a counselor: "A good marriage counselor will help a couple talk about the reasons for cheating in terms of the marriage and about the problems that lead a partner to seek an extramarital relationship. In counseling, the couple discuss what they feel the marriage lacks or where the rough spots are, and then with the counselor's help they work to correct their problems."[1]

Almost any book, magazine, or newspaper advice column dealing with this issue reinforces this view of affairs as caused only by problems in the relationship. Following are some typical examples: "Cheating always points to a weakness in your relationship."[2] "Ask yourself why you need to go outside the marriage, what is lacking in your relationship."[3] "Affairs are then attempts to meet important needs that are unmet within the context of the marriage."[4]

Sometimes affairs are explained in terms of the inability of a person to control their behavior. In *Every Other Man*, author Mary Ann Bartusis suggests: "Some men seem unable to remain faithful. I believe this is because they suffer from emotional deficiencies."[5] And in her book *Back from Betrayal*, Jennifer P. Schneider writes of affairs as a sexual addiction.

The tendency of the experts to focus almost exclusively on personal failure and inadequacies strongly reinforces the personal view of affairs. And this interpretation contributes to the difficulty of being able to fully recover from the emotional impact of this experience. Despite the fact that 85 percent of the members of BAN had sought some kind of counseling, many expressed disappointment with the help they had received. Most of them continued to struggle with unresolved feelings for many years following their experience.

Of those who stayed in the marriage, most were involved in an ongoing battle with their painful feelings about their spouse's affair. Those who got out of the marriage fared no better. Some had been divorced for quite a long time, but were still plagued with feelings of bitterness and resentment. Others, who'd had affairs themselves, had been unable to recover from their sense of guilt and regret—especially when it had cost them their marriage and, in some cases, their relationship with their children.

THE LANGUAGE OF AFFAIRS

Another reason we see the issue of affairs only in personal terms is because our entire vocabulary for discussing affairs reinforces this perspective. The standard words are blaming words and serve to inflame the already raw emotions this issue stimulates. And, unfortunately, many of the books dealing with this subject use words that contribute to the problem. The trio of words used most often are *adultery, infidelity,* and *betrayal.*

The words *adultery* and *infidelity* reflect a personal assessment of the person who has an affair as an adulterer or an infidel. In one recent book dealing with this issue, the words *cuckold* and *infidel* were used throughout the book to refer to the people involved in this situation. Being labeled a *cuckold* feeds into the feelings of shame and embarrassment felt by someone whose partner has an affair. And being labeled an *infidel* is an extreme moral judgment of a person that places all the blame on their shoulders while ignoring other factors.

We have only to look at other words that have been used to label people to understand their significance. Through the years there have been many examples of the damage done by the words used to refer to certain groups of people. Most of us cringe at the thought that we once used words like "retarded" or "deaf and dumb" or "Mongoloid." The negative impact of this kind of language is undeniable in retrospect. It's irrelevant that there may have been no specific intention to inflict pain or create difficulty for the people involved; that was, nevertheless, the effect.

The word *betrayal* has been especially popular in books on the subject of affairs, with three recent books using it in the title. It might not seem obvious just why this is a problem. But the word *betrayal* implies that the person having an affair is fully aware of the pain this will cause their partner and proceeds to "betray" them anyway. This reinforces the idea of personal blame and adds to the difficulty of coping with the emotions and gaining a broader understanding of what has happened and what to do about it.

We need to raise our awareness of the impact of words and make a conscientious effort to diffuse the personal pain caused by the language we use to discuss affairs. Because of the power of words to affect the way we think, this book deliberately avoids the long list of judgmental, blaming words so common to the language of affairs.

The authors of *American Couples*, Philip Blumstein and Pepper Schwartz, also expressed their recognition of the importance of the words we use to describe this issue: "We have purposely chosen the word *non-monogamy* when we write about sex outside a couple's relationship. We would prefer to use a less clumsy word, but this is the only word that is morally neutral: It neither condemns nor condones. We need a word that merely describes; therefore, we have intentionally omitted expressions like *cheating*, *infidelity*, and *adultery*, except when the couples we interview use them to express the way they feel."[6]

In explaining the choice of the title, *Adultery*, for her book, Annette Lawson acknowledges the importance of the words used to address this issue. She consciously used the word *adultery* to reflect the fact that her study was based on addressing the "sinful" connotation historically attached to this issue: "There is almost no academic work by historians, sociologists, or anthropologists that focuses on adultery and no book with the word *Adultery* as its title. I wanted to speak of adultery for two reasons: first, I wanted not to avoid but to point to its long history as sin and crime and, further, to dramatize the greater sin, the greater punishment inflicted on the married woman."[7]

THE LEGACY OF THE MONOGAMY MYTH

The unresolved pain from dealing with affairs is primarily due to the effects of seeing monogamy as the norm and affairs as a personal failure to fit this norm. As discussed earlier, the basis for this belief is a myth. While it's extremely difficult to overcome strong emotions with rational understanding, we need to take a closer look at the evidence that monogamy is not the norm in our society. This involves examining our sexual habits as they relate to our ideas of monogamy.

One significant pattern of behavior is that of divorce and remarriage, which we've come to call "serial monogamy." Not only is there a change of partners at that time, but usually a number of sexual partners between marriages. Since approximately half the population goes through this process, it's a strong challenge to our ideas of long-term monogamy.

The other serious threat to monogamy, of course, is the number of people involved in affairs. Earlier, I used the conservative estimate of 60 percent of men and 40 percent of women at some point engaging in extramarital affairs. But we need to take a closer look at the statistics on affairs to determine what they can contribute to an understanding of our sexual patterns.

While affairs happen in nonmarital, committed relationships as well as within marriage, most of the statistics deal only with *extramarital* affairs. These statistics began with Kinsey's reports in the 1940s and early 1950s. Kinsey's samples included 5,000 men and showed that by age forty, 50 percent of the men had experienced extramarital sexual intercourse.

Two studies during this decade dealing exclusively with men indicate a continuous increase in the number of men having extramarital affairs. *The Hite Report on Male Sexuality* of 1980, surveying 7,239 men, found 72 percent of men married two years or more had had sex outside of marriage. Jan Halper, author of the 1988 book *Quiet Desperation,* reported on the results of interviews with 4,000 men and found that 82 percent of the sample had had extramarital affairs.

The increase for women having affairs has been even more significant. In *The Extramarital Connection,* sociologist Lynn Atwater's book about women having extramarital affairs, she reported: "It is among women, more so than men, that rates of extramarital participation are rising dramatically."[8] This observation is born out by the soaring statistics.

Kinsey's original samples of 6,000 women showed that by age forty, 26 percent of the women had experienced extramarital sexual intercourse. Morton Hunt's 1972 survey showed that 52 percent of divorced women had had an affair, many of those coming during the last few years of the marriage. *Cosmopolitan* magazine's 1980 survey of 106,000 readers (employed women between the ages of eighteen and thirty-four) reported that 50 percent had had at least one extramarital experience. For those over age thirty-five, it jumped to 69.2 percent. And Shere Hite's 1987 report of 4,500 women in *Women and Love* found that 70 percent of women married five years or more had had sex outside of their marriages.

These recent statistics, both for men and for women, are extremely high and legitimately debated, but many people question *any* statistics on extramarital affairs, arguing that statistics are unreliable and confusing and that no one knows precisely how prevalent affairs are. While there are slight differences in the estimates based on clinical studies and questionnaires, the bottom line is compelling in showing an extremely high (and rising) incidence of extramarital affairs. These statistics (especially when combined with the number of serial marriages, which provide a variety of partners) illustrate that our old view of monogamy as the norm in our society is a myth.

Despite the statistics, there are still ways to interpret them that can bring a false sense of security. For instance, in his book *Private Lies*, Frank Pittman says, "Monogamy [is] practiced by most of the people most of the time." While he acknowledges, "Infidelity in over half of all marriages is a lot of infidelity," he diminishes it by adding, "Many adulterers have only one affair, and much of the infidelity takes place in the last year of a dying marriage."[9]

Since monogamy lies at the heart of our longings for certainty and security, it's scary to admit that things are not the way we desperately want them to be. So people are looking for just this sort of reassurance that they don't need to be concerned about this problem. Unfortunately, this attitude also discounts the significance of this experience for those couples who have dealt with it personally. The fact that it *did* happen (regardless of how many affairs or for what period of time) has far more impact on the relationship than the fact that a spouse may have been monogamous "most of the time."

For the person who knows their spouse has had an affair and is still trying to understand why, acknowledging the prevalence of affairs in our society can help them put it in a more realistic perspective. Understanding just how many others face the same situation (regardless of who they are or who they're married to) can help break the sense of being so alone, isolated, or singled out for this experience. It can help overcome the feeling of "why me?" People who have not yet faced this issue, either in their own lives or with their friends or family, would do well to start with a realistic picture of the frequency of affairs in society as a whole. It's not that the sheer frequency means it will happen to any specific person, but it does say a lot about the kind of support to expect from society for remaining monogamous vs. having affairs.

The issue here is not whether monogamy is natural, or whether people are *naturally* monogamous or *naturally* not monogamous. That's a useless debate, as was clearly expressed by Jessie Bernard in her classic work, *The Future of Marriage:* "Millions of words have been used to document both the naturalness and the unnaturalness of monogamy. The question . . . is, actually, unanswerable. We will never know if there is anything intrinsic in human nature that limits the ways the sexes can relate to one another because no one has ever survived outside of any culture long enough to teach us. Human nature seems to be able to take almost any form of marriage—or unable to take any form."[10]

We can only understand monogamy and affairs in a societal context, in terms of the attitudes of society as a whole. Normally, when we try to understand why affairs happen we look only at the reasons why a person might *want* to have an affair, such as the excitement of sexual variety. But this doesn't explain why affairs *happen*. People may want to have affairs for a wide range of reasons, but their decision to act on those desires is affected by the values and actions of those around them.

Affairs happen in so many marriages that it's unreasonable to think they're due solely to factors within each marriage. Whatever the personal factors involved in affairs, they are more than outweighed by the significant, powerful, and pervasive societal factors. We have a responsibility to learn more about our role, individually and as a whole, in supporting these societal factors that contribute to affairs.

2

· · · · · · ·

How Society Contributes to Affairs

The ability of people to recover from their experience in dealing with affairs would be significantly improved if they recognized that this is not just a personal issue, but a societal issue as well. Since one of the principles of the Monogamy Myth is that society supports monogamy, it's been difficult to recognize the many factors in society that contribute to affairs. We can't change our attitudes about affairs or our actions that inadvertently support them without an understanding of these societal factors. Let's look more closely at some of the most important ones.

LEARNING TO LIE ABOUT SEX

One of the most basic of the societal factors contributing to affairs is the general dishonesty about sex that exists at all stages of our lives. Our parents are seldom honest with us about sex when we're growing up. Very few children get good information about the physical aspects of sex. And almost none of us gets sound information about sexuality and sexual love. As teenagers, we continue this pattern of secrecy by presenting a false image to our parents when we first become sexually active. When a teenager is dating and is supposed to avoid sexual intercourse (but they want to do it), they usually wind up doing it in a secretive way, while pretending to their parents that they're not.

By the time a person gets married, they have had plenty of

practice at being deceptive and dishonest about sex. So when a person is married and is supposed to be monogamous (but they want to have sex with someone else), they often go ahead and do it in a secretive way, while pretending to their spouse that they're not. When faced with a decision about monogamy or having an affair, their only prior experience in dealing with this kind of sexual conflict was to sneak around and secretly do what they wanted, while pretending they weren't.

When one woman discovered her husband had been having affairs for ten of the fifteen years of their marriage, she was overwhelmed by the contrast to his "faithful husband" image during that time. It seemed impossible that he could have been so deceptive. But it's easier to understand when we realize that this kind of pretense is what we learned as teenagers hiding our sex lives from our parents. When a married person has a secret affair, they're simply continuing the pattern of deception learned while growing up.

Just as our parents didn't question us directly about their suspicions when we were teenagers, most of us don't question our mates directly about our suspicions of affairs. At all stages of our lives, the primary way we deal with sexual issues is to close our eyes and hope for the best. This kind of conditioning to be deceptive is an important factor in understanding why affairs happen.

THEM VS. US

Another factor that contributes to affairs is the conditioning we get as little children about how to view the opposite sex. While it varies on an individual basis, the overall tendency has been to isolate us into two opposing groups. By the time we grow up and get married, we've learned to lump all members of the opposite sex into a group of *them* as opposed to *us*. We don't simply see each other as different, but as somehow strange, mysterious, and suspect—not quite to be trusted.

Much of the way we see each other is based on stereotypes of what it means to be a man or a woman. Despite the strides made in overcoming some of the stereotypes, our conditioning is still very strong. Men have been conditioned to see women as weak and emotional, while women have been conditioned to see men as important sources of attention and approval. Men tend to see women as *sex* objects and women tend to see men as *success* objects. These images create distance and misunderstanding between individual men and women.

When women get together and discuss men, they invariably talk about them in general, stereotypical terms. They commiserate with each other on the frustrations of dealing with men: They won't talk, they won't share the housework, they don't remember special occasions, they watch sports on television all the time, they don't send flowers or love notes, they don't listen to what you have to say, they don't call when they say they will, they always want to hang out with "the guys," they're preoccupied with their jobs, they always look at other women when you're out together . . . .

Men have their own set of complaints and often engage in moralizing conversations with other men about how women are: They're emotional, they're preoccupied with their looks, they're never on time, they spend too much money on clothes, they take too long with their makeup, they're always fussing with their hair, they want you at their beck and call, they spend too much time shopping, they get upset when you look at "men's magazines," they want you to account for every minute of your time . . . .

These gripes may seem petty on the surface, but there's an underlying importance. They all create distance between men and women, making it easier to think of each other in stereotypical terms instead of as individuals. This in turn makes it more comfortable for men and women to deceive each other and rationalize having affairs.

ROLE EXPECTATIONS

As a society, we have certain expectations of the roles to be played in the husband/wife relationship. The restrictiveness of these marital roles can make us more vulnerable to affairs where we can "be ourselves." An affair represents newness, variety, freedom, and fun. There are no responsibilities or distractions from being fun-loving, playful, and affectionate. When people are in affairs, they're seen as exciting individuals with very special qualities. And the ordinary world with its many concerns and responsibilities doesn't intrude on this separate world of affairs.

On the other hand, their marital roles are so filled with responsibilities (financial, children, social) that couples often come to see each other primarily in terms of the functions they perform in the marriage. It's not uncommon to hear a married couple refer to each other as mother and father even when their children are not present. They tend to identify so much with the roles that they lose sight of the person behind the role.

Herb Goldberg drew attention to the dysfunctional nature of this kind of male/female relationship in his book *The New Male Female Relationship:* "The old roles have become too poisonous for any truly conscious and sensitive person to accept. A new blueprint is a necessity lest men and women cement themselves into hardened postures of mutual antagonism and alienation."[1]

SEX FOR SALE

The commercialization of sex through advertising also contributes to affairs in our society. Women, particularly, are used to sell almost every product on the market. Most ads promoting the good things in life imply that a sexy-looking woman is part of the package, one of the "good things" a man deserves. This constant bombardment of ads depicting women as sex objects makes it very difficult for men to relate to women in any way other than sexual. Overcoming this one-dimensional view of women requires a deliberate effort, and an essential part of changing this perspective is recognizing the subtle but powerful influence of the way advertising promotes the view of women as sex objects.

It's not just "men's magazines" that portray this sexy image of women. The advertising in women's magazines is also blatant in its depiction of women as sex objects. As for the impact of this advertising on women themselves, it provides a constant, subtle pressure to *be* one of these sexy, desirable women. The constant barrage of flawless models leads most women to feel ugly by comparison. This fits into their fears that their partner will find someone more attractive and have an affair. One of the first things a woman does when she suspects her partner of having an affair is to focus on her own appearance. And advertisers are only too happy to reinforce this insecurity by trying to sell her all the things required to compete with other women.

One impact of this concern about attractiveness is that it increases the likelihood that a woman will have an affair. Many women see an affair as validation of their attractiveness, serving to bolster their confidence about their appeal and their ability to attract men. One woman confided in me that she'd had several affairs, but had never had orgasms with anyone but her current husband. She hadn't engaged in the affairs for sex, or even for companionship; she did it strictly because she felt better about herself by virtue of having men want her. And by the time they wanted her badly enough, she had sometimes gone too far to feel she should stop them. Unfortunately, this is not an unusual situation.

So living up to the ideal presented in the media for being desirable has a direct impact on many women who take the advertising messages to heart. They invest a lot of time and money in pursuing the images portrayed in the media. Then when they succeed in getting the reaction promised by the ads, they're not prepared to deal with it—and wind up having an affair.

THE FAIRY-TALE MARRIAGE

Another element in society that has the effect of encouraging affairs is the idealized image of love and marriage that most of us are conditioned to expect. This view of marriage is presented in the media, in romance novels, and in self-help books on how to find the ideal mate. When we get married and find that this fairy-tale version of marriage is untrue, we become disenchanted and look for this kind of romantic love in an affair. We keep hoping that somehow, somewhere, there is the perfect partner for us—if only we're lucky enough to find him or her.

We're vulnerable to this kind of influence because we get very little realistic information while growing up. Most people pretend their marriages are far better than they really are. Our parents and other adults usually protect us, if possible, from knowing the truth about how difficult it is to sustain a satisfying love relationship. Many times their marriages are real disasters, but we may be so preoccupied with our own world while growing up that we don't pay much attention. Then it can come as a shock when we discover years later that their whole relationship had been a pretense.

The traumatic impact on a young adult of their parents getting divorced after many years of marriage was depicted in a segment of the television program "Thirtysomething." When Ellyn's parents announced they were getting a divorce, she was devastated. Despite the fact that she had her own separate life (with a successful career, a live-in love relationship, and a host of good friends), the news of her parents' divorce created an overwhelming sadness and disturbance in her life. Even though there had been earlier indications of problems in her parents' marriage, she hadn't wanted to see them. Instead, she clung to the ideal image of how she *wanted* their marriage to be.

Clearly, we have held unrealistic images of marriage, not only in general, but specifically in terms of our own parents and of previous generations. Again, Herb Goldberg reflects on this situation in *The New Male Female Relationship:* "Most couples bond in romantic euphoria, evolve into a deadened interaction, and separate with feelings of alienation and sometimes concealed rage or open hatred. The relationships of the past never really worked to the benefit of both partners. At best, they were functional adjustments, compromises, or accommodations to social pressures."[2]

The hope for a happy marriage, both for ourselves and for those close to us, is a deep longing in our society. Even with all the statistics on divorce and extramarital affairs, many couples still cling to the romantic ideal of marriage. By holding an unrealistic image of marriage as a magical union where people live happily ever after, they often ignore the possibility of attractions to others or deny feelings of suspicion of an affair. This attitude inadvertently contributes to the climate that makes affairs more likely.

A LITTLE HELP FROM MY FRIENDS

Ironically, a subtle kind of support for affairs is the excitement of discussing this taboo activity with friends. Since society is still less tolerant of a woman having an affair than of a man, it's seen as somewhat more of a risk for a woman to share this kind of secret.

Most women only feel safe to tell their closest friends. But the reinforcement that comes from the excitement of telling others can increase the positive feelings about having an affair. And it sometimes carries the extra bonus of having her friends see her as a more interesting person because of this aspect of her life.

One woman found that flaunting the fact she was having an affair with a much older, successful man was the only way she felt really special. She didn't have any particular personal qualities that made her stand out, but she was able to garner attention just by telling stories about her "friend." The saddest part of this effort for attention, however, was the fact that it gradually became known that she had been painting a very biased picture of the relationship. In fact, it had become hurtful and demeaning, the only real pleasure being the satisfaction she got from being able to talk about it with her friends.

Talking with friends about their affairs is an even more powerful factor among men than among women. There's a general acceptance of affairs among men, so they don't fear being criticized by other men. Women are usually unaware of the degree of openness with which men discuss their affairs with each other. We tend to think all they talk about is business and sports, but that's just when we're around. When we're not around, they also talk about sex—specifically their affairs. Just as in high school, they don't talk about sex with their steady (or in this case their wife or primary partner); they share information about their "outside" sex.

In the years since *Beyond Affairs* came out, I've had some interesting conversations with men about this aspect of their lives. Several men who stopped having affairs (after they were discovered by their wives) described how they missed the camaraderie of talking about their affairs with other men. While we usually don't see this kind of male sharing, there was a rare chance to observe this behavior on an "Oprah Winfrey" program where the entire audience was made up of men (both married and unmarried) who had had affairs. The general atmosphere was one of being at a sports function as they cheered each other on in their comments about affairs.

This peer support for affairs plays a very special role for most men. They would find it frustrating if they were unable to talk about their experiences with friends. While they get a lot of satisfaction from the affairs themselves, they also get a great deal of pleasure from impressing their friends with stories of their adventures.

While men generally find acceptance (and often a certain status) among their peers for having an affair, there's an interesting twist in that it only applies to a man "successfully" having affairs, meaning having them without his wife finding out. As long as she doesn't know (and supposedly isn't being hurt), his image remains intact, with a certain pride in handling it so well. But to get caught and bring pain to his wife is seen as a failure, both by the individual man and by his peers who previously accepted, even applauded, his affairs.

FASCINATION AND TITILLATION

Whenever there's a report in the media about someone having an affair, it invariably becomes big news; most people want to know as many of the details as possible. There's a certain fascination with this subject and a measure of enjoyment derived from vicariously being a part of it. Romance novels and soap operas glorifying affairs usually enjoy a high degree of success and popularity. And affairs are a staple subject of magazine articles, newspaper columns, movies, and television shows (either as a movie-of-the-week or the topic of a television talk show).

While we may be quite judgmental of people having affairs, at the same time we often behave in ways that would seem just the opposite. In most instances, the pleasure in focusing on this issue is not obvious, but it's quite noticeable in observing the audiences of television talk shows dealing with the subject. While members of the audience clearly verbalize their belief in monogamy and their intolerance of affairs, they also laugh a great deal about the subject and clearly enjoy the titillation of the discussion.

For example, here's an excerpt from a television talk show where the host is questioning a guest who has admitted to having extramarital affairs:

Host: "You're married twenty years?"
Guest: "Yes."

Host: "And you fooled around for how many of those years?"

Guest: "All of them."

At this point the audience erupts in laughter. And it's not a one-time instance; this response is repeated many times throughout the program. Of course, some of it may be nervous laughter, but the general climate in the studio is not serious in the way one might expect when discussing such a universally condemned activity. The expressions on the faces of the audience show they are clearly enjoying the proceedings.

This is not an isolated instance on just one talk show; it's the standard pattern whenever the subject is affairs. So we have a situation where people are condemning it with their statements and condoning it with their behavior. This schizophrenic attitude toward the issue is one of the factors that contribute to affairs and is a major drawback to addressing the issue in a responsible way.

THE CODE OF SECRECY

• • • • • •

The most significant support for affairs in our society is the secrecy that surrounds them (and our infatuation with that secrecy). Because of the stories of famous people involved in affairs and the way affairs are paraded before us every day in movies, television, and newspapers, there might not appear to be so much secrecy surrounding them. But where it really counts, in an individual's own life, there's still a tremendous amount of secrecy. In fact, there's a code of secrecy in our society that involves all of us and affects every aspect of this issue.

The basic attitude of the general public is that you can't talk about affairs. And closely aligned with this assumption is the belief that you *shouldn't* talk about them. Since many people see affairs as wrong, they feel that secrecy is appropriate. But by adopting this attitude, we are providing the kind of protection and support that actually increases the likelihood of affairs.

The code of secrecy provides a buffer from the world that makes it easier for a person to engage in affairs and to avoid dealing with the consequences, or even to seriously contemplate the consequences. We can't expect those who are having affairs to be more concerned about the effects of their behavior as long as the secrecy we all support serves to protect this kind of behavior.

There are a number of very specific ways secrecy protects the person having an affair: If their partner suspects, they're less likely to question them directly. If friends or coworkers know, they're less likely to tell the partner. If their mate finds out, they're less likely to tell other important people (mother, children, or the clergy). The person having an affair comes to count on this co-operation in maintaining the secrecy to which they are totally committed.

Never tell. If questioned, deny it. If caught, say as little as possible. This is the basic code of secrecy among those having affairs. They don't stop to question why this is the accepted motto; it just is. It may come partly from a natural human drive toward survival and self-protection. It's understandable that they don't want to be discovered and have to deal with the consequences, so most people will go to great lengths to deny it and to avoid any efforts to discuss the subject of affairs.

The advice most people offer to a person considering telling their spouse about their affair is, "Don't." The experience James had when he decided to tell me about his affairs is fairly typical. When he confided his intentions to a friend, the friend's response was to plead with him not to do it. The friend felt sure it would be the end of the marriage. But James knew I already suspected and felt that openly acknowledging it before I confronted him would give us a better chance of sustaining the marriage; and he was right. But the friend's warning was in keeping with the general belief in secrecy when dealing with affairs.

PROFESSIONAL SUPPORT FOR SECRECY

Surprisingly, this attitude of secrecy is reinforced by the standard advice from marriage counselors, therapists, and advice columnists. Many of them are adamant in their belief that a person shouldn't tell their partner about an affair. The following statement by Melvyn Kinder and Connell Cowan in their book *Husbands and Wives* is typical of this advice: "As a rule of thumb, we never advocate confessions, for the harm they may do is all too often irreparable."[3]

Most of the BAN members felt quite differently about this issue. They expressed a great deal of frustration about the professional posture against telling of an affair.

> *It angered me so much to hear a professional encouraging a man to live a lie. He called in to her talk show and asked how to get his wife to trust him. He had had an affair and wanted to be honest, so told her and desired to reestablish a real relationship with her. She really put him down; said he'd made a terrible mistake in telling his wife. I wanted to explain to her how much better honesty was for me than wondering.*

This has been my own experience as well, that honesty is preferable to the years of suspicion and doubt. But it's a point with which many therapists disagree, and one that surfaced as an issue when James and I appeared as guests, along with a therapist, on "Bill Boggs Midday," a television talk show in New York in 1980. The therapist strongly advised against telling a partner about an affair, saying there was too much risk that the marriage would end. Bill Boggs, the host, was just as strong in pointing out the irony and unfairness of acknowledging the high percentage of people having affairs and at the same time saying we can't disclose those affairs and deal with them.

James and I described our own experience as an example of being able to tell about affairs and work through the situation to develop a better relationship. But the therapist dismissed our experience as being unusual. She said we were unique, that most couples would not be able to do what we had done. I don't feel that way and don't want others to be discouraged just because they might not feel capable of facing this issue at the moment. I know how much people can change. There was a time in the early years of James's affairs when we would not have been able to talk about them and work through it, but we worked toward the day when we *were* able to do it—and this is the hope I would offer to others. It's a growing ability that can be developed by anyone who wants to strive to develop a relationship based on honesty.

This is an effort worth pursuing, because the caution against the risk of telling about an affair ignores the fact that there's also a risk if it's *not* disclosed. In marriages where affairs are kept secret, certain topics of discussion are avoided because the deceiving partner fears being discovered and the other is reluctant to appear suspicious. This causes many relationships to be dominated by dishonesty and deception. It's doubtful that a couple can keep something like this hidden for the rest of their lives without a terrible strain developing. A large part of the high divorce rate may be due to the alienation caused by the dishonesty inherent in affairs, even if the affairs are never confronted.

So while some relationships come apart from not being ready to deal with the truth, many more relationships come apart because of the effort to keep an affair hidden. And even if the marriage doesn't end in divorce, it's likely to become empty and meaningless because of so much secrecy. It may be that there is no escape from the pain, regardless of whether the affairs are kept hidden or exposed. Often it's just a matter of time before either the marriage becomes a pretense or the truth comes out, along with the pain it brings.

This is not meant to diminish the pain of finding out. But one of the advantages of volunteering the information about an affair instead of waiting until it's unexpectedly discovered is that it allows a degree of preparation that can significantly reduce the pain of finding out. The person doing the telling has a responsibility to take steps to increase the likelihood that the disclosure will lead to building a closer relationship rather than tearing it apart.

First of all, they need to be motivated by a desire to improve the relationship, not a desire to unload their feelings of guilt. They also need to be prepared to hang in and work through their partner's reactions to the information, regardless of what those reactions may be. And it's important that they plan the timing of their disclosure of an affair. They need to consider such things as their partner's general level of self-esteem, what other issues or pressures their partner is currently dealing with, and whether their partner has a clear understanding that they are loved. The first task of the person who plans to disclose an affair is to attend to preparing their partner to be able to hear what they have to say.

Perhaps the most critical factor in determining the impact of this disclosure is having an understanding of affairs in the context of society as a whole. For instance, if a person is told of their mate's affair—and they see it only as a personal reflection on them and strictly as a personal failure on the part of their mate—they're likely to feel the devastation that has been so typical of this situation.

However, if a person is told of their mate's affair—and they recognize that it is *not* a reflection on them personally and that their mate is not *solely* responsible for its happening—they're much more likely to be able to hear it and deal with it in a way that leads to improving their lives in the long run.

As more professionals include this societal perspective in their work with couples seeking their help, they may be more inclined to encourage responsible disclosure as a way of working toward building a relationship based on honesty. There are indications that some therapists have come to believe in the need to overcome our secretive way of dealing with affairs. One therapist who supports the importance of honesty is Frank Pittman, author of *Private Lies*. Another professional who has written extensively about the importance of honesty is John Powell. In his book *The Secret of Staying in Love*, he makes a compelling argument for honesty as the basis for achieving the kind of relationship most people want.

> Some say that you cannot be totally open and honest with those you love. It would destroy them. These people say that we need only to be real in the part of ourselves that we do reveal. I do not believe this.
>
> Each person must make a fundamental judgment about the stability, the depth of understanding and acceptance in the relationship involved. The presumption is that these communications should either be made now, or, if that would seem imprudent, then the revelation should be made at some time in the future when the necessary depth of understanding and acceptance have been achieved. Permanent withholding will always be a permanent deficiency in the relationship, an obstacle to the love that could have been.[4]

Unfortunately, most professionals who discourage disclosure of an affair also discourage too much discussion once an affair is discovered. A typical example of this advice can be found in Joseph and Lois Bird's book *Marriage Is for Grownups:* "Once the couple have decided to rebuild their marriage, the first sensible agreement is not to discuss the affair any further. This is the only rationale, yet many couples have difficulty sticking to such a decision."[5]

This is also the approach taken in advice columns like the one by Carol Botwin in *New Woman* magazine: "Don't ask your husband why he had the affair. Instead, open up communications about your marriage, without referring to the past."[6]

The members of BAN consistently reported their difficulty in dealing with professionals who held this attitude. Here's a report I received from one meeting regarding the consensus of the group on the need for more honesty and discussion about affairs after they are discovered.

> *What came across loud and clear were two things. First, that counseling hadn't helped. Counselors had not encouraged the hours necessary of talking and openness to get over the pain—just forget it and go from now. Next was the same need from all for honesty about everything. Honesty is the key. Willingness to face it all. Only then did it seem that we could build and trust again. I think the "professionals" or "experts" need to go through the issue of affairs to really understand how it feels when we find out.*

There were also some reports of professionals who went so far as to suggest that a person is somehow inadequate or wrong for not being able to get over their feelings more quickly.

> *What the counselor failed to do was to let me get out my feelings. Every time I said what I felt, the counselor said I had no right to feel that way.*

> *My therapist is telling me that my recurring questions are possibly a subconscious excuse for me to get out of my marriage or else I could let go of them.*

> *Two months after this all came out I was told that there was something wrong with me because I hadn't let go of it. The therapist is saying, "Stop feeling self-pity." Is it really that easy? I need reassurance that my feelings are not so unusual.*

There's an irony in the professional attitude against too much discussion of an affair. In dealing with most interpersonal issues, there's general agreement about the importance of talking things through. In business, the ability to discuss differences and solve problems is seen as essential. Good parent/child communication is recognized as vital to being an effective parent. And sharing is touted for couples in dealing with most issues; but when it comes to affairs, professionals tend to see prolonged discussions as interfering with being able to put the past behind and move on to the future.

This attitude fails to recognize that if it's not dealt with, it just gets buried alive—and may keep coming back to haunt them for the rest of their lives. People need to continue talking until they get enough understanding to be able to *genuinely* leave it behind. Also, sometimes it's easier to deal with the facts than the fantasies. While each person must decide what information they want and whether they are ready to handle everything they might find out, they have a right to ask about any aspect of their partner's affair they're curious about.

It's natural to want to understand something as significant as this experience usually is for most people. I recall how critical it was to my recovery to spend the long hours talking through the issues. I was not trying to get even or to get out of my marriage. I was simply trying to understand what had happened, to make some sense of all the confusion I felt at that time.

CONSEQUENCES OF THE CODE OF SECRECY

One of the major consequences of the code of secrecy is the way secrecy compounds the problem for people trying to cope with their partner's affairs. The secrecy leaves them alone with their anxiety if they suspect and alone with their pain if they find out. It's quite possible that this isolation threatens a person's sanity even more than dealing with the affairs themselves. Chapters 3 and 4 describe the feelings of desperation of people struggling alone with their anxiety, confusion, and pain.

The secrecy makes it considerably more difficult to get information and understanding about the "nonpersonal," societal factors involved. Without this information, people can't put their experience into perspective, so they continue to see it primarily as a personal failure. This becomes a vicious cycle that keeps them suffering in silence, which is why most people carry the emotional burden of this experience for the rest of their lives.

Despite the consequences of abiding by the code of secrecy, it's seldom that anyone even considers doing otherwise; but ignoring the code of secrecy can lead to a very different outcome. In one instance, the wife of a prominent businessman, family man, and community leader caught her husband having sex with his secretary on his desk. Instead of taking it personally and hiding it while she licked her wounds and decided what to do, she proceeded to talk openly about what had happened. It was not a very large community and soon virtually everyone knew the story. As you can imagine, the impact (both on him and on her) was significantly different from what it would have been had she abided by the more socially accepted code. She avoided the "pitiful" stereotype and showed she was a strong, confident person who recognized this was not a reflection of her worth as an individual or as a wife. And her husband had to face the consequences of his actions and share responsibility for dealing with the situation.

This may be an unusual way of reacting to this experience, but it illustrates how a lack of secrecy can alter the way the issue affects the people involved and the perceptions of others. If people cannot count on the code of secrecy to protect them, they may change their thinking—and their actions. And the other party will certainly feel stronger and be able to recover more quickly since they won't have to hide their head in shame, hoping others don't find out.

Most people personally dealing with affairs will continue to be controlled by the code of secrecy until there's a change in society's attitude. We can't expect them to share their fears or suspicions as long as we consider their silence to be appropriate behavior. A careful look at the impact of our silence indicates a need to redefine *appropriate*. It's certainly appropriate to try to alleviate the pain and anxiety of those who are suffering alone as a result of our silence.

The next section focuses on "The Experience" of personally dealing with affairs. Fortunately, we don't have to go through it ourselves in order to learn from the experience of those who have faced this issue in their own lives. A clearer understanding of the pain caused by our personal view of affairs can be a motivating force for changing our attitudes and our behavior.

PART II

· · · · · · · ·

THE
EXPERIENCE

3

Suspicion and Confrontation

The experience of dealing with affairs begins with dealing with the *suspicion* of an affair. Because of the personal view of this issue, someone who suspects their partner of having an affair usually tries to deny their suspicions and to find ways to rationalize their concerns. It also causes them to keep their suspicions secret, both from their partner and from others.

I clearly remember the strain of hiding my fears during the years I suspected my husband of having affairs. This is typical behavior for a woman who suspects her partner, but men are even more likely to try to keep others from knowing if they suspect their wife of having an affair. For many people, keeping their suspicions secret becomes a major drawback to being willing to confront the situation. The strength of this commitment to secrecy is one of the reasons that going from the first signals of an affair to the final confrontation is such a slow, painful process.

Men are more likely to move through this process at a faster rate than women. But some men delay the confrontation simply because they're unable to imagine their wife having an affair. While women are more likely to believe it could happen, they often avoid a confrontation because they don't know how they'd handle it if they found out for sure. Some people, both men and women, confront their partners as soon as they have any suspicion of an affair. But for most, coming to grips with their suspicions is a long struggle.

FIRST SIGNALS
· · · · · · ·

I am afraid that my wife is having an affair. There are those gut feelings and small clues and things that strike you wrong.

I simply can't shake the feeling that he's hiding something from me. I can't put my finger on exactly what it is, but I can't help wondering if he might be having an affair.

This is the first level of suspicion—that gut feeling that something is wrong. Most people reported having this feeling, although it varied in the way it appeared. For some it was a sudden feeling that resulted from a casual comment or incident, while for others it came as a growing feeling of uneasiness.

INTUITION

These first signals are seldom the stereotypical things like lipstick on the collar or strange phone calls. They're usually much more subtle, more of an intuitive reaction to changes in a partner's behavior, a sense that "something is different." Following is a list of some of these changes:

- more distant
- more preoccupied with job, home, or outside interests
- more attentive to clothes and accessories
- more focused on weight and appearance
- more absent from home with time unaccounted for
- more glued to the TV set than usual
- more interested in trying new things sexually than before
- less attentive
- less willing to talk or spend time together
- less available emotionally
- less interested in family issues
- less interested in sex than usual
- less involved in shared activities

It's tempting to look at this list, find that many of the items fit your partner's behavior, and jump to the conclusion that they're having an affair; but it's not that simple. Determining whether or not there's any significance to the changes in behavior depends on evaluating both the number of areas of change and the degree of change. For instance, changes in only a few areas would not be as significant as changes in many different areas. And very slight changes would not be as significant as more drastic ones. But even if there has been a great deal of change in a large number of areas, this does not *necessarily* signal an affair. There are many reasons for such changes in behavior that have nothing to do with affairs, one of the most likely being an increased level of stress in the work environment. Other possible causes include concerns about health, aging, family, or finances. Unfortunately, the possibility of an affair is so frightening to most people that they either suppress their awareness of these changes or rationalize that they are temporary, or insignificant, or due to some problem that will just "go away." Whether or not the changes are due to an affair, they indicate a problem that needs to be discussed.

Typically, however, people don't act on intuition alone, without additional evidence. For example, one woman (we'll call her Kathy) became aware of a great many changes in her husband's behavior in a short period of time and concluded that they were due to job pressures. He had said nothing to indicate that the stress at work had increased, but since he was working longer hours and was preoccupied much of the time he wasn't at work, she concluded that this was the case. She didn't check out her assumptions because she knew her husband didn't like to discuss his work and she didn't want to upset him by questioning him about it. (Of course, she also didn't want to upset herself by focusing on her fears that he might be having an affair.) The denial of these first intuitive feelings of the possibility of an affair is very common; but, as we'll see later, they often prove to have been a reliable first signal.

CASUAL COMMENTS OR INCIDENTS

Another possible first signal is a comment or incident that seems harmless on the surface, but is felt as an indication that something is wrong. This was my own experience—an overwhelming feeling of anxiety as a result of an incident that didn't *seem* to warrant such a strong reaction. Here's the way I described it in *Beyond Affairs:* "One night soon after [James] got home we went to another couple's house for dinner. The other man worked with James and the four of us had been friends for quite awhile. When we arrived at our friends' house, James kissed the other woman hello. I felt a rush of anxiety. I didn't know what was wrong, but it was like a warning light going off in my head. We'd been married for eleven years and this was the first time he'd kissed another woman like that."[1]

Many years later when I learned the details of his affairs, I found that this incident had happened a few days after he began his very first affair. Here's the way James later explained his behavior: "My kissing Janet that night had no special significance in relation to her. I simply had a new, expansive outlook toward the world. I felt more warmth toward everyone . . . and I started expressing my feelings more directly—especially with female friends."[2]

On a gut level I had sensed something was wrong without any clue as to what it was. While the incident was not directly related to his affair, it was a clear first signal that something had happened.

In the case of Kathy (who had attributed her husband's behavior changes to job pressures), there came a time when her husband began making casual comments about how helpful his secretary was in helping him handle his job. Kathy felt relief that he was saying *something* about his job situation and took this as proof that his behavior changes had been due to his concern with responsibilities at work. She recalled feeling some twinges of anxiety at his praise of his secretary, but tried to discount those feelings as part of her effort to rationalize his behavior.

RATIONALIZATION

• • • • • •

When my fears and doubts and suspicions started, I couldn't or wouldn't believe this could happen to me. I started looking for little things that would prove it was not happening. I have tried to understand how I became so unable to trust my instincts and so unwilling to challenge my spouse.

One of the major reasons people rationalize their early suspicions of an affair is because they don't want to believe it's true. The sense of personal shame and embarrassment that comes with entertaining the possibility that this could happen causes them to look for ways to convince themselves that their suspicions are unfounded. Most people will go to great lengths to rationalize their concerns about an affair.

Kathy's experience provides a good example of the power of rationalization. She had managed to suppress her intuitive feelings about changes in her husband's behavior and her anxieties about his comments about his secretary; the next stage was to rationalize the tremendous increase in the number of hours he put in at the office. He said he was involved in a difficult project that required working many nights and most weekends. Their family time was being significantly reduced and she was concerned about the impact on the children, but she *wanted* to believe him. So she rationalized that he was just having a hard time at work and that she shouldn't make it more difficult for him by challenging what he said. It was somewhat easier for her to reach this conclusion because of her belief that he was a good husband and father, not the type to have an affair.

RATIONALIZATIONS BASED ON MYTHS AND STEREOTYPES

One of the reasons people don't trust the first signals of an affair is because they conflict with many of the myths and stereotypes they've accepted about who's at risk for having an affair. There's a tendency to think affairs happen only to certain kinds of people. Following are a few of the false assumptions we make about who will and who won't have an affair:

She won't have an affair if she's a devoted mother (and therefore wouldn't do anything that might hurt the kids). Being devoted to her children doesn't preclude having an affair. In fact, many women (who might otherwise divorce) stay married "for the sake of the kids"—and have an affair on the side.

He won't have an affair if he has strong religious convictions. I vividly recall one woman's anguish as being particularly severe as she described finding out about her husband's affair. "He was a pillar of society, big church man, never did anything wrong. I've been devastated." Her shock was even greater because of having assumed he was not vulnerable.

She won't have an affair if she's not particularly attractive. Since people generally look more attractive to a new person (and sexual interest tends to heighten people's attractiveness) this is a very poor rationale. In fact, if a spouse doesn't find their mate attractive (and a stranger does), it may make it even *more* likely that an "unattractive" person will have an affair than a more secure, "attractive" one.

Affairs happen only within a few specific professions. Many people feel safe as long as their spouse is not in a "glamorous" profession that has traditionally been associated with affairs, such as being an actor, a musician, or a sports figure. This is the attitude of those who see affairs as a problem exclusive to people who work in a unique professional environment. But affairs affect people from *all* walks of life, not just those with high visibility.

Affairs happen only among people who travel. This is closely related to the previous stereotype about affairs happening only in certain professions. Salesmen, truckers, professional athletes, and others who travel extensively are considered prime candidates, and those whose spouses don't fit that profile breathe a sigh of relief. Fewer women's jobs call for travel than men's, but many men are adamant about their wives' not traveling, because they believe this is the best way to prevent them from having an affair. While traveling may make affairs easier to hide, they are certainly not restricted to those who travel.

Affairs happen only among the rich or powerful. Some people have been misled by hearing of so many well-known people having affairs; they begin to think of affairs as relegated to people with special opportunities by virtue of their money or prestige. As long as *their* spouse isn't a business tycoon or a politician, they think they're relatively safe. This, however, is another false stereotype based on efforts to categorize people who have affairs.

Most of us actually know very little about the subject of affairs. What we think we know is made up of myths and stereotypes that often bear little resemblance to the actual facts of the situation.

Since there has been so little clear thinking about this issue prior to facing it, and since it's extremely difficult to think clearly in the midst of such emotional turmoil, most people fall back on these stereotypes when trying to cope with their fears. This only contributes to their tendency to rationalize their concerns and to keep their partners from knowing of their suspicions.

RATIONALIZATIONS BY THE PERSON HAVING AN AFFAIR

It's clear that rationalization is not limited to the one who *suspects* an affair. The person *having* an affair also uses rationalization to avoid facing the impact of their behavior. Unfortunately, when the suspicions are kept hidden, it makes it easier for the person having an affair to avoid thinking about the consequences of their actions. As long as they can ignore any potential problems, they feel okay about themselves and feel safe in continuing their affairs, despite the risk of pain to their partner or damage to the relationship.

One of the most prevalent rationalizations by the person having an affair is, *what they don't know can't hurt them*. If their mate's suspicions are not being expressed, they tell themselves that their mate doesn't know. But many people who seemingly don't know about their partners' affairs are simply pretending. They *do* suspect it's happening and they *are* hurting. Sometimes they just don't know what to do about it; so they do nothing.

Another rationalization is that if the spouse never suspects the affair, then no damage is done. This belief ignores the fact that the distance and isolation created by the deception of an affair cause a great deal of damage to the relationship. People become strangers who don't really know each other. This makes a couple vulnerable to all kinds of problems and pressures that can eventually lead to divorce or a deadened relationship.

For both partners, rationalization is a way to avoid facing reality. And the process of rationalization often grows more ironic as time goes on. Once people get caught up in it, they become capable of manipulating their thinking in any way that will allow them to avoid confronting the situation. But this delay leads to an increase in dishonesty on both sides, and it tends to compound the difficulty when the confrontation finally takes place.

DENIAL
· · · · · · ·

At some point, rationalization fails to be sufficient to explain the behavior of a person who suspects an affair. When there is actual evidence to suggest an affair and they still fail to confront it, they have entered the stage of denial. This is what happened to Kathy. Her husband's practice of working long hours had continued for several months. Kathy normally did not go to his office because they had an understanding that it didn't appear professional to have wives show up at work. But one Saturday morning when she needed to get in touch with him and there was no answer when she called his office, she decided to take the children and try to find him.

By this time she had become much more suspicious that he was having an affair (although she had not made a clear decision to confront him). When she arrived at his office, she saw his car parked in the parking lot, but there was no answer when she knocked on the door. She didn't have a key, so she continued to knock and call out her husband's name. When he finally unlocked the door, he emerged with his secretary, both of them looking flushed and disheveled. When Kathy said, "How could you do this to me," he denied any wrongdoing and instead attacked her for spying on him and accusing him unfairly. She felt shaken and confused, and took the children and ran from the awkwardness of the situation. She didn't know what to do or what to think and actually began to doubt her own sanity. She dropped her accusations at that point, but it was only a temporary lull leading to the final confrontation, which we'll discuss later.

The longer a person denies their suspicions, the harder it becomes to face them. They become immobilized by their fear and confusion, sometimes spending years avoiding a confrontation.

WHEN TO CONFRONT
• • • • • • •

It's important for each person to face the issue of affairs only when they're ready. This is a very individual decision that each person must make for themselves. A person's feelings about confrontation are likely to be different at different stages. For instance, being slightly suspicious for a short period of time is far more tolerable than a growing suspicion that continues for several years. The length of time and the intensity of the feelings frequently dictate a person's decision as to when to confront their suspicions of an affair.

But these are not the only considerations. Sometimes a person hesitates to confront their partner because of the fear that a *false* accusation might push their partner into an affair.

I'm afraid to question my husband because if I'm wrong it might encourage him to go ahead and do it.

I wanted to speak of my suspicions but didn't, as I was told if I kept it up I'd have something to be suspicious of.

The threat of somehow "causing" an affair by voicing suspicions is an understandable fear if someone constantly questions or repeatedly accuses their partner of having an affair without any evidence that it's happening. But whatever risk there might be in falsely accusing a partner is not nearly so great as the risk of failing to address the issue until it becomes a serious barrier to communication and trust. Unfortunately, the overwhelming feeling of a person who suspects their partner of having an affair is fear, the fear of falsely accusing their partner if they're wrong and the fear of facing the facts if they're right. Their need to know the truth is squashed by the fear of knowing it.

DO YOU *REALLY* WANT TO KNOW?

A person needs to be sure they really want to know before asking if their partner is having an affair. One of the biggest drawbacks to being ready to confront the suspicions is feeling unprepared to face it if the suspicions turn out to be true.

*I'm so afraid to ask about it, for fear I'll hear the worst. I try to
block it out of my mind because I guess I just can't face the reality
of the situation.*

One woman told of her efforts to avoid knowing about her husband's affair as being similar to her little girl's desire to play "let's
pretend." She found it easier to just *pretend* it wasn't happening
than to find out for sure. She recognized that she really didn't want
to know at that time. What she wanted was some reassurance that
he wasn't having an affair. But if a person is only looking for
reassurance, this is likely to be detected by the person having an
affair (who is already convinced it can never be discussed). As a
result, the reassurance is likely to be given—but it's likely to be
false reassurance.

As time goes on, without good information, people tend to imagine the worst; and at some point they desperately want to know
where they stand and what they can count on. Here's the way some
of the BAN members expressed their feelings about this need to
know whether their suspicions were true.

*This lady is really tormented by not knowing. My imagination has
been wonderful! In fact, if my husband really did everything I imagined, he would truly be the Incredible Hulk.*

*Nothing can be worse than all these years of not knowing what's
going on and where I stand.*

Another factor that affects whether a person wants to know of
their partner's affair is whether they think others know about their
suspicions. Since self-esteem is so integral to this whole dilemma,
a person who knows friends or family members are aware of their
suspicions may feel pressure to "save their pride" by confronting
it before they're ready. They may think as long as no one else
knows, it's as if it's not happening. But when others know, they
can't pretend it's not an issue.

This means that friends or family members need to be very
sensitive as to how their involvement might affect the situation.
Basically, they should avoid any efforts (either openly or subtly) to

pressure a confrontation. They should wait until there's an indication that the person who suspects really wants to know before saying anything at all. And even then, the most helpful involvement might be to express their understanding that an affair is not a sign of personal failure or personal inadequacy. This kind of support can allow a person to feel more capable of facing their suspicions, making them better prepared to confront the situation.

DO YOU FEEL OPEN TO *EITHER* STAYING OR LEAVING?

I will not get a divorce just because he had an affair, nor will I remain married just because he promises never to do so again.

An important consideration as to whether or not a person is ready to confront their suspicions is their willingness to remain open to either staying in the relationship or leaving it. If their decision is predetermined (whether the decision is to stay or to leave), then they're not fully prepared to deal with the issue of affairs.

This is where a societal perspective of affairs becomes so critical. If a person takes the personal view of affairs, they may feel compelled to get out of the marriage if they discover their suspicions of an affair are true. But if they get beyond the strictly personal interpretation of what has happened and understand the societal factors involved, they can assess their situation and their prospects for the future and make a conscious decision as to whether to stay or leave. Unfortunately, people who see only the personal view of affairs tend to think that leaving will help them overcome their pain, when, in fact, it's not leaving (or staying) that heals the pain, but *understanding* more about affairs that will bring this kind of recovery.

On the other hand, if a person feels they simply must stay in the marriage (even if their suspicions turn out to be true), they're also unlikely to recover from the emotional impact. It would be better for them to delay confronting it while they work on whatever factors lead them to believe they have to stay. Frequently, these factors are practical considerations, causing a person to feel trapped in the marriage. Chapter 9 includes a discussion of these practical factors that play an important role in making this decision.

So the bottom line is that a person needs to work through all the factors that may influence their decision rather than just dwelling on their suspicions. It's also better for a person to avoid actively trying to validate their suspicions unless and until they're ready to confront them. For instance, if someone feels they would have to confront their partner if they got absolute proof of an affair (and they don't feel ready to confront), then it would be self-defeating to sneak around trying to get evidence of an affair. But at the point that someone feels prepared to validate their suspicions and explore the possibilities of either leaving or staying, they're probably ready for a confrontation.

If we look at Kathy's experience in dealing with her suspicions, it becomes clear that this was a critical factor in the way she handled her situation. When she encountered her husband and his secretary at his office and he denied any involvement, she didn't pursue it further at that time because she needed to think through her feelings and try to gain more strength before confronting it. Within the next few months she did a lot of thinking about their relationship, her feelings for him, and the possibility that they could work through it if her fears turned out to be true.

When she arrived at this point (being clear that she wanted to know and being prepared to leave or to stay), she felt ready to face it. So she managed to get a key to his office and slipped in one weekend morning when he was out of town and no one else was there. She was prepared to go through his desk and his files—whatever it took to satisfy herself about her suspicions. She was amazed at how easy it was to find evidence. She found receipts from hotels and restaurants for times he supposedly was somewhere else, but more importantly, she found notes from the other woman that left no doubt they were having an affair.

She felt weak and scared when she had the proof and found she was not nearly as prepared as she had thought. She didn't feel capable of a personal confrontation, but she wanted him to know she knew about the affair. So she wrote him a note saying simply, "I know," and signed her name; she left it on his desk on top of the papers she had discovered. Then she took the kids and went to her parents' home to sort things out for herself.

In this instance, the couple did stay together and rebuild their marriage on a basis of honesty. Kathy's husband was not prepared for the emotions he felt when he realized she knew of his affair. He had assumed he'd never be caught and hadn't imagined the pain this would cause. He was afraid of losing her and the children, and he set about doing everything possible to address the problem and save their marriage.

HOW TO CONFRONT

. . . .

There is no way to guarantee the reaction to a confrontation, but there are some ways to improve the chances that it will lead to resolving the suspicions about an affair. The approach to be used depends on what stage of suspicion has been reached. When there's an intuitive sense that something is wrong based on behavior changes or casual comments or incidents that seem unusual, it's reasonable to express a concern about them without specifically questioning an affair. This makes it possible to learn if there is some other problem that needs attention.

But if a partner's response is that "there's no problem" or "nothing's wrong," this is unlikely to be reassuring. While it doesn't necessarily mean an affair is being hidden, it does increase the likelihood that something significant is wrong. And if the partner's reaction to expressions of concern about the relationship is one of irritation and impatience, this is likely to increase the feeling that they're having an affair.

As the suspicions continue (and perhaps grow stronger), most people eventually reach the point of asking more questions. Unfortunately, the ambivalence most of them feel about wanting to know but being afraid to find out causes their questions to be tentative. And since the basic code of secrecy of those having affairs is to deny it whenever questioned, any tentative questions will almost certainly be met with denial.

I suspected that something was going on, but when I asked some very tentative questions, he said he loved me and couldn't believe I was questioning his trust.

This kind of response is seldom reassuring to the person who feels anxious and uncertain about what is going on in the relationship. In fact, the nature of the response to their questions may serve to increase their fears of an affair. For instance, one man (who was only mildly concerned prior to asking his wife if there was something wrong) became much more concerned due to her reaction to his questions. She became very agitated and began crying and saying he should know she would never do anything to hurt him. The intensity of her response caused his concerns to grow stronger, but it succeeded in stopping his efforts to discuss it further—at least for the time being.

One possible reason for such a strong reaction is because this is an effective way to stifle further conversation. While there are exceptions, of course, the intensity of the reaction often corresponds to the validity of the questions. For instance, as the suspicions of an affair grow stronger and the questions become more probing and more frequent, the denials of an affair are likely to become more vehement. Here are some illustrations of this kind of situation.

What do you do when all the signs are there, but the husband ridicules you, gets angry with you, ignores you, and refuses to admit he is having an affair?

I felt in my gut for the past two years that there were other women, but he said it was totally ridiculous and I was imagining things—I really thought I was losing my mind.

He tells me I have no reason to be insecure, no reason to be suspicious, that these things I feel and think I know are all my imagination. So he reinforces my feeling that I'm crazy.

When the denial includes an attack on the person asking the questions, especially when it includes trying to make them think they're crazy for being suspicious, it's more likely that the suspicions are true. A harsh response may be an attempt to bring any additional questioning to a halt. When someone isn't trying to hide something, they are more likely to respond in a calm (perhaps even comforting and reassuring) way; but a person who has something to hide is more likely to react defensively and make accusations in return. When someone is absolutely clear about the honesty of their response to a question (whether it's about affairs or some other issue), they do not feel threatened and do not feel the need to be defensive or critical. It's the lack of confidence in their own integrity that usually causes this kind of overreaction.

Sometimes the anxiety of wondering about a partner's affair becomes overwhelming and a person finally decides on a direct confrontation. If tentative questions have produced denial (and possibly even anger), it's essential to be absolutely direct in order to have the best hope of getting an honest answer. This literally means asking the question, "Are you having an affair?"

However, if the confrontation is to have the best possibility of succeeding, this question should not be blurted out without proper preparation. If the question comes as a complete surprise, it may prompt a knee-jerk denial. First of all, it's important to choose a time and a place where there will be no intrusions or distractions. Then it's essential to establish real contact with the person; look them in the eye and say something like this: "I need an honest answer to the question I'm about to ask you. I hope the answer is no, but I need to know the truth. If the answer is yes, that's not necessarily the end of the relationship. But if it's no (and I find out later you were lying), I'm not sure we would be able to overcome that."

A failure to ask this kind of direct question allows the other person to avoid a direct reply. Many people having affairs depend on never being asked directly, on never having to lie. A straightforward question makes it more difficult to pretend no harm is being done and to deny the possibility of getting caught and having to deal with the consequences. Of course, even making this kind of direct effort doesn't guarantee success in getting an honest answer; some people are accomplished liars and this won't have as much impact on them. It can be extremely frustrating to finally ask directly, and still feel the truth didn't come out. It's at this point that people usually stop talking and start taking more direct action aimed at finding out the truth for themselves. At this point, entrapment may feel like the only alternative.

The kind of entrapment that Kathy used to confront her husband doesn't always work out so well. The embarrassment and anger of the spouse who is trapped sometimes causes them to be unwilling to try to work things out, regardless of what the other person wants. So entrapment can backfire if there's to be hope for staying together, but when it comes only after other efforts to confront the issue have been tried and have failed, it's a reasonable course of action.

Entrapment that involves a private investigator or other outside source is even more likely to cause the trapped person to react by pulling away completely. The person may begin to feel like a victim, which may overwhelm any feelings of guilt they might have had about their behavior, leaving them with little sympathy for the problems they have caused. This may not matter to the person who suspects an affair, however. If they have been unable to resolve their questions without resorting to this kind of entrapment, they may have reached the point of caring only about "capture and punishment," and no longer have any interest in saving the relationship.

One man who had become obsessed with finding out whether his wife was having an affair resorted to spying on her and following her everywhere she went. His suspicions were finally validated when he caught her with another man. But at that moment, he felt such overwhelming fear, anxiety, and pain that he felt incapable of facing her and confronting her with the truth. In order to save his own sanity, he felt he had to leave and never even talk to her about it—and that's what he did. So the end of his suspicions also brought an automatic end of his marriage.

AVOIDING SUSPICION AND CONFRONTATION
· · · · · · ·

Being suspicious and confronting those suspicions can be a complicated and difficult process, and most of us would like to avoid ever being in this position in the first place. But at some time almost everyone worries about their partner being tempted to have an affair. That's a reasonable concern—almost anyone can be *tempted* to have an affair. Attractions to others are natural and not a cause for alarm. It's what we do about the attractions that matters. And this is where, as we've seen, the attitudes and behavior of society as a whole play such an important role. But what we do as individuals can also make a difference, for better or for worse. Unfortunately, some of the most common things people do to try to prevent affairs are extremely ineffective.

Some people think they can somehow threaten their partner into not having an affair. The most common ultimatum is, "I'll leave you if I ever find out you've had an affair." There are two problems with this kind of statement. First, the key words "if I ever find out" just let the person know they need to be especially careful not to get caught. And second, if an affair does take place, the one who made the threat may not want to carry it out, but may feel honor-bound to do it anyway. It's never wise to threaten just what you'll do in any given circumstance. What people find over and over is that whatever they *thought* they would do turned out to be quite different from their actual reaction. Any absolutes can become a complicating difficulty in trying to deal with a very complex situation.

Another ineffective way some people (especially women) try to avoid having to deal with suspicions about affairs is to say that if their partner has an affair, they don't want to know about it. There are several reasons this is both dangerous and damaging to the relationship. It's dangerous in that the unavoidable impact on the other person is to feel they're not really expected to be monogamous, that on some level there's an understanding they'll probably have an affair. This has the effect of increasing their openness to that happening. So the process of saying you don't want to know increases the chances that it will happen.

Several men who were having affairs told of their relief at the fact that their wives had made it clear they didn't want to know about any affairs if they happened. The men felt a strong responsibility to keep their wives from knowing, but they felt no responsibility to avoid having affairs. They felt there was an "understanding" that it was acceptable as long as it was done discreetly and any public embarrassment was avoided. For this reason, such a statement is damaging to the image of the person being deceived as a full and equal partner in the relationship. And it's damaging to the relationship beyond just the dishonesty it encourages about affairs, since it indicates a willingness to tolerate dishonesty in general.

Couples who tacitly agree to a lack of honesty (thinking it will never be fully exposed) find they feel quite differently when faced with the consequences of their dishonesty. The pain that comes from learning of a partner's affair is often compounded by the full awareness of the depth of the dishonesty and deception that exists between them. Affairs are only one of many issues that couples fail to be honest about; and the more areas that are kept hidden from each other, the more distance there will be between them, and the more reason there will be for suspicion.

4

· · · · · · ·

The Pain of Knowing

A person who finds out for sure that their partner has been having an affair is likely to feel overwhelmed with emotions—pain, anger, embarrassment, resentment, bitterness, and a sense of loss. Despite the degree of suspicion or the nature of the confrontation, no one seems to be fully prepared for the pain of knowing the truth. One woman described how she had known it instinctively for a long time, but was still devastated when her husband told her he was having an affair.

The initial reaction when people first face the reality that their partner has had an affair is likely to be a physical one. They tend to feel disoriented, lightheaded, and weak in the stomach.

> *I am sitting here with a kicked-in-the-stomach, tight-hard-to-breathe, screaming headache feeling that won't go away.*

> *My surprise and pain were so great that I nearly went into shock—I couldn't eat and couldn't sleep without medication for months.*

Since the Monogamy Myth is so pervasive, people don't acknowledge the possibility of having to deal with this issue, so they're totally unprepared when it happens. We need to hear the pain of these people in order to fully appreciate the damage being done by our current ways of understanding and dealing with affairs.

Pain, oh my God yes, and hurt beyond belief. Sometimes I would get up from a chair and look behind me, astounded that it was not filled with blood, because I felt that I was bleeding, the pain was so great.

I have had nightmares, have become hysterical, and cried until I don't know where all the tears came from. I feel betrayed and like a part of me has been killed.

One of the specific pains a person must deal with following the discovery of their mate's affair is the thought of their partner having sex with someone else. In a later chapter, we'll look more closely at the impact on a couple's sex life and explore ways to achieve sexual healing. But the sexual impact, like all the other effects of an affair, takes a long time to overcome.

The immediate challenge for most people is simply getting through each day. In many instances, people feel so weak and depressed that they find it difficult to function. They sometimes isolate themselves from the rest of life, as if nothing else exists. They lose interest in their job, their family, and their outside activities. One woman described how she felt so shattered and disillusioned that she became a confused vegetable. And another saw herself as being insecure and vulnerable, like a baby learning to walk.

Unfortunately, this happens just as they need a great deal of energy to cope with the issues they face. They can't begin to recover until they get enough physical strength and vitality to sustain them through this period of emotional devastation. Most people fail to appreciate the importance of taking care of the basics: exercise, nutrition, and relaxation.

Exercise is one of the best sources of energy—and one of the most effective ways to deal with overwhelming emotions. Getting the body in motion usually results in a sense of well-being that is difficult to achieve in any other way. That's because exercise does more than just mysteriously make us feel better. There's a physical change that takes place, causing the better feelings. Aerobic exercise actually causes the release of a natural chemical in the body similar to the kind of artificial chemical people take in pill form to make themselves feel "high." When we exercise, we don't just think we feel better, we actually do feel better because of this chemical change in our bodies.

This physical route is the one most often taken by men in dealing with their emotions. They may literally wear themselves out physically so they're too tired to feel the pain. In fact, they may use exercise as a way to mask the feelings that continue to lie beneath the surface. At some point they will need to talk about those feelings and come to grips with them, even if they can't do that at first.

On the other hand, a woman is more likely to talk about her feelings but less likely to turn to physical activity. She usually feels listless and depressed, and the last thing she wants to do is exercise. Mainly, she wants to get in bed and pull the covers up over her head, which, of course, does nothing to help her feelings. Instead, she usually gets a sluggish headache that makes her feel even worse. What she needs is to get out and start moving as soon as possible.

Nutrition is another basic problem for people who are dealing with the stress of an affair. The impact of stress on the body is widely known, and this is certainly a time of intense stress in the lives of most people. Because of that stress, the immune system is weakened and there's more susceptibility to sicknesses of all kinds. That's why it's all the more important that nutrition not be overlooked. But typically, the appetite just disappears. Here's the way one woman described it.

The way things have been the past six weeks, if I can eat, it's a miracle—and if I can keep down what I've eaten, then it's the Second Coming.

Even when eating is resumed, it's likely to be junk food or "mood food," whatever food represents some sense of comfort. This is particularly a problem for women who have typically used food in this way. While it may be inevitable that there will be some problems with eating, a person needs to be conscious of the importance of nutrition in order to have the energy they need to simply get through the day, and hopefully avoid getting sick.

Relaxation is another important factor in dealing with the stress of this situation. But most people look for ways to escape the reality of trying to deal with their partner's affair by turning to alcohol, drugs, tranquilizers, sexual activity, or just sitting like a zombie in front of the television set. Unfortunately, these do nothing to diminish their stress, increase their energy, or improve their self-esteem. Instead, these activities usually make their lives even more difficult. They need to find more natural ways of relieving their tension, such as meditation, relaxation tapes, religious services, or simple things like watching sunsets or water scenes if that's available.

The strength of the emotional impact on the person whose partner has had an affair makes it extremely difficult for them to think straight. As soon as they feel they will survive physically, most people desperately try to figure out what happened—but they usually feel that none of it makes sense. In struggling to understand how their partner could have had an affair, they inevitably ask the practical question of how their mate could have taken the *risks:* the risk of getting caught, the risk of venereal disease, the risk of pregnancy, the risk of hurting the family, the risk of divorce. This willingness to risk so much not only creates problems in understanding, but it can also become a source of resentment.

What I resent is that he did exactly what he wanted to no matter what the risks (and they were high). He risked everything because he wanted to have affairs.

As difficult as it may be to comprehend, in most cases the person having an affair simply doesn't think about the risks involved. They just assume nothing will ever go wrong. Even the additional risk of AIDS doesn't guarantee an end to the problem of affairs. It will serve as somewhat of a deterrent in that it's likely to affect the choice of partners. But many people will ignore this risk in the same way they've ignored all the others. Affairs are extremely exciting for most people, a heady experience that exists outside of the normal distractions of life's problems. And this excitement simply blocks out the focus on whatever risks might be involved.

WHEN A PERSON WON'T TALK

• • • • • • •

One of the most frustrating parts of dealing with the fact that a partner has had an affair is the incredible difficulty in getting them to talk about it. This is one of the first issues for most couples following the discovery of an affair—that the spouse who had the affair won't talk. Apparently, they are willing to do almost anything or have almost any consequence rather than discuss their affair.

Sometimes it's very predictable that a person won't talk. For instance, one man who felt sure his wife was having an affair and felt they could work through it and stay together simply couldn't get his wife to discuss it. He felt this was because he'd told her when they were married that he'd divorce her immediately if she ever had an affair. And no matter what he said now, he was unable to reassure her that he no longer felt as he had when he issued that threat. Since there may be no way to escape the effects of such statements once they're made, it's important to avoid making these kinds of threats; they inevitably reinforce the general reluctance to talking.

The basic resistance to talking is not as mysterious as we might think. There are five primary reasons people won't talk about their affairs once they've been discovered: a belief in the basic code of silence, a desire to maintain their self-image, a belief that it's best for their partner not to know, a desire to avoid the emotional reactions, and a desire to continue having affairs.

BELIEF IN THE BASIC CODE OF SILENCE

The main reason for not talking is because of the basic code of silence that is implicitly understood by anyone having affairs: "Never tell." "If questioned, deny it." "If caught, say as little as possible." The power of the code of silence often presents an impenetrable barrier to communication that can be absolutely maddening to the person who desperately wants to know why the affair happened.

> *I've asked and asked and asked. I've written to him to try to get him to talk, but he won't—and it's driving me crazy.*

She finally admitted she had had an affair, but I simply cannot get her to talk about it. I don't know how much longer I can stand her silence.

It's clear that the secrecy in dealing with affairs is a critical factor in a person's struggle to recover from the emotional impact of this experience. But the person who refuses to talk about their affair is acting on instinct, supported by the general assumption (as discussed in chapter 2) that this is the appropriate course of action when an affair is discovered.

FEELINGS OF GUILT AND SHAME

Another reason for not talking is much more personal. It relates to a person's desire to see themselves as okay. Self-esteem is an important factor in anyone's ability to successfully make their way in the world. By accepting responsibility for a mate's pain, a person becomes vulnerable to feeling bad about themselves.

All I get from my husband is to leave him alone. I really think he is on a guilt trip himself and can't stand to face the pain he's caused. He can hardly bear to look at me.

I can see she is still struggling within herself. I know there are still some painful emotions built up in her.

My husband is a man of few words. I think that he would just as soon forget this "affair" business ever took place.

The person who has an affair usually wants to avoid thinking about the effects of their actions. Their feelings of guilt and shame tend to increase with the amount of discussion about it, so they prefer to keep it as quiet as possible. Another way their guilt is increased is by having other people know about the affair. It's hard enough for them to deal with their spouse knowing, but they can't imagine having to face the fact that their mother or their children or people within their religious community know about it. So they may be quite adamant about insisting that it not be discussed with others.

As discussed earlier, most people already feel a terrible dilemma about admitting their mate's affair to others, so their spouse's attitude reinforces their own uncertainty. The concern about protecting their mate's image (as well as their own) frequently means a person will decide to avoid confiding in others. Unfortunately, this interferes with their getting the support they need to be able to come to grips with what has happened and cope with their feelings about it.

PROTECTING THEIR PARTNER'S FEELINGS

When I ask for information, she says, "I don't know—I don't remember," or "Please let's not do this to ourselves."

One reason many people don't want to talk about their affairs is that they genuinely believe it's best for their partner not to know too much. But when a person discovers their mate is having an affair, their world suddenly turns upside down. In order to recover any sense of balance, they need to get more information and understanding of the situation. Without answers to their questions, they convince themselves that the answers must all be bad; otherwise why wouldn't they be told what they want to know. They feel they're being treated like a child, and they resent it.

If the information didn't exist, it wouldn't be so frustrating and demeaning. But they know their partner has it and simply refuses to give it to them. This makes a balance of power in the relationship impossible. So even though a person may say their refusal to talk is for their mate's own good, it doesn't help. It's doubtful if trust can ever be restored in a relationship where this persists.

I remember how tough it was on James when I continually asked more and more questions. Intellectually, I wanted to move on and get over it, but emotionally I needed the ongoing support and understanding he gave me. It was extremely important that he never said, "Enough is enough, let's get on with our lives." Of course, nobody would choose to go through the thousands of hours of talking about this if there were some other way. In my own case, I think it was an essential part of overcoming my feelings and finding peace of mind.

AVOIDING A SHOWDOWN

While they are reluctant to admit it, another reason for not talking is simply that they don't want to deal with their mate's emotional reactions. As stereotypical as it may sound, women who have affairs don't want to deal with the possibility of a physically violent reaction from their husbands, and men don't want to deal with the likelihood of a torrent of tears from their wives.

> *My husband tells me he loves me, tells me he is not unhappy with me, tells me there is "nothing wrong" with me. But he sits mute when I express my feelings of pain and fear and general inadequacy.*

> *She will say she wants me to tell her when I am feeling down, but when I do, she turns away and tries to change the subject.*

The desire to avoid these emotional reactions includes a desire to avoid involving other people. Many wives are afraid their husbands will confront the other man, and most husbands are afraid their wives will tell all the details to friends or family. So it's not just the emotions of their spouse that people don't want to deal with; they also don't want to deal with the reactions of others. Also, if others are not brought into the issue, they feel they don't have to really look at the situation—or do anything about it.

A DESIRE TO CONTINUE HAVING AFFAIRS

The most disturbing of the reasons why people won't talk is one they seldom admit openly—that they have no intention of stopping their affairs, and it's a distraction to the enjoyment of them if they have to deal with their spouse's reaction. Even if they stop temporarily, it's much easier to resume their old ways as long as the issue is not discussed. This is one of the reasons it's worth *trying* to get a person who has had an affair to talk about it.

NO EASY ANSWERS
· · · · · · ·

No matter how much time and energy a person puts into the effort to get their partner to talk, it's still quite possible that they won't succeed. If they simply cannot get the answers they want about their partner's affair, they need to find a way to accept this situation. It usually takes a long time to reach this point, since most people continue trying to get their spouse to talk long after it's clear that their efforts are in vain. One woman who had tried for almost two years to get her husband to discuss his affairs finally accepted the fact that he was never going to talk about why it happened. It was easier for her to accept this situation once she realized that there may be no clear reason, that even the person having an affair may not know exactly why it happened.

There are no easy answers about anything related to the issue of affairs. That's why it's so important to learn as much as possible about all aspects of this issue and avoid any quick or simplistic solutions. It's understandable that a person wants to overcome the initial pain of learning of their partner's affair as quickly as possible, but sometimes the most effective way of doing that is to accept an unavoidable period of adjustment. While it's extremely difficult to cope with the strong emotions during this period, a conscious effort to hang in and deal with each aspect of the situation may allow for a more satisfying resolution in the long run.

DEALING WITH THE THIRD PARTY
· · · · · · ·

The third party is an unavoidable focus, especially during the early period of dealing with affairs. For the person who has been having an affair, the third party is a source of "unfinished business." They must tell the third party of the mate's knowledge of the affair and decide whether to end it. As for the person who discovers their mate's affair, the third party often becomes the focus of a great deal of anger and curiosity.

I have quite a struggle letting go of the rage I've felt toward the man my wife had an affair with.

My anger and humiliation caused me to secretly hope she would die, or get married or somehow be totally unavailable.

It's understandable that the third party becomes the target for a lot of the anger and rage people feel at this time. This is in keeping with the general attitude in society that sees the third party as responsible for much of the misery brought about by an affair. While we have been quick to condemn and criticize the third party, we've also tended to have an exaggerated image of them as a femme fatale or a Don Juan. If the third party is completely unknown, a spouse may become consumed by fantasies about this stranger in their mate's life and want to find out as much as possible about them.

SEEKING CONTACT WITH THE THIRD PARTY

The desire for information about the third party often includes wanting to see them and talk to them. This is much more likely to be the case with women than with men, since women have been trained to deal with interpersonal issues by talking through unresolved questions or feelings. Men, on the other hand, don't have this conditioning to verbally process their thoughts and feelings. So unless they want to confront the other man physically, they are not likely to want to meet him. Not surprisingly, while many wives want this face-to-face contact with the other woman, their husbands invariably disapprove.

My husband wants to know how "normal" it is for the wife and lover to want to get together and talk. His lover and I have talked a few times. I don't know what her reason for wanting this may be, but I did it for information.

In a kidding manner, I threatened to talk to the other woman's husband. It almost sent him into orbit, and I think he conveyed this to her and panic set in for her too. Shed a lot of light on things for me.

When a woman decides to seek out the other woman, she's obviously taking a chance on being hurt even more if the meeting goes badly. One woman who made contact with the other woman greatly regretted her decision. At first the other woman wouldn't accept her calls, but she persisted. Finally, she met with the other woman, but the meeting was nothing like she expected (or hoped for). The other woman was not the least bit embarrassed or guilty about the affair. She flaunted details of places they had gone and things they had done together. She chided the wife for being so naive and trusting, and said she felt sure she knew her husband better than his wife knew him. Not surprisingly, the wife felt even worse after this encounter, which only served to increase her feelings of anger and frustration.

Since there's no way to predetermine the outcome of meeting the other woman, each person must decide for herself what she thinks is best. While it might be a mistake for some, for others it might work out very well. It can diffuse the intensity of their feelings and give them a sense of the real person behind the image of "other woman." In one very unusual case, the wife eventually developed a close personal friendship with the other woman (after the affair was over). Here are some other examples of good results from this kind of contact.

I had an incredible need to meet one of them. I arranged to meet one head on and she represented all the others for me. My meeting was very beneficial to me. Every person must do what they must do. For some it would be disastrous. For me it was right—very good.

I had a talk with the woman my husband had the affair with. Since we talked, I feel so relieved. I ended up feeling sorry for her.

I felt I had to contact the woman. (I hadn't known her except by sight.) I realized it meant exposing myself to her, but I didn't care what she thought at that point. I had to see her as a fallible human being, not the monster I had conjured up. It worked! She even seemed understanding.

Getting rid of the image of the third party as some kind of monster can be very beneficial in allowing a person to let go of the anger and hatred that may have been consuming them and keeping them from using that energy to work on their own healing. Another purpose that may be served by this kind of face-to-face meeting is that it can restore a sense of pride to the wife who has felt inadequate. Confronting her adversary in person can give her a sense of strength that offsets her feelings of being weak and helpless. It can clear up the misconceptions that invariably exist if the other woman was a stranger prior to the affair. And it can diffuse some of the negative emotions that result from seeing the other woman *only* in that role without knowing anything else about her. One of the most beneficial results of such a meeting is that it can serve to eliminate the fantasy that the third party is someone with whom a person can't possibly compete.

SOMETHING SPECIAL

One reaction that many people have upon discovering their mate's affair is to wonder how they compare with the third party, hoping to find ways to feel superior (or at least not inferior). A person's assessment of the third party is often exaggerated, causing them to think the third party has some exceptional qualities that they are lacking. They tend to focus on whatever might be considered "special" about the third party.

The biggest hangup I had was that the other woman was so much younger and very thin.

I never knew my wife was so impressed with power and success. He certainly wasn't anything to look at, but apparently she didn't care.

These examples demonstrate the grain of truth in the stereotype that men are attracted to women's looks and women are attracted to men's success. But it would be a mistake to assume that these are the only factors that determine the attractions to a third party. In most instances, there is nothing particularly special about the third party, but I know from my own experience how often we torture ourselves by dwelling on whatever special things we can identify about the affair.

When I found out about James's affairs, I identified a number of special things that made them difficult to deal with. First of all, there was the specialness of his first affair, because it was the first time he'd ever had sex with anyone but me. Somehow, this seemed especially significant. It was as if we had this "pure" sexual relationship (having both been virgins when we became sexually involved with each other) that was now ruined. I also had to deal with the fact that he learned to enjoy oral sex during one of his affairs before it became an integral part of our sex life. And I found that I was bothered by the idea that some of the women were very large-breasted.

In reflecting on the fact that my husband had about fifteen affairs over a seven-year period, I don't know whether dealing with so many third parties made it easier or more difficult. On the negative side, it could have soured me on women in general. It could have made me suspicious and judgmental toward all women. But it didn't. It somehow forced me to look beyond the particular individuals, thus diluting the feelings that usually get directed at one person. I came to see the importance of the role they played instead of looking only at the individual.

PLAYING THE PART

The third party is seldom superior to the spouse; they're simply different—and the primary difference is just that they have the role of *lover* instead of the role of *husband* or *wife*. Allen Wheelis wrote an extraordinarily vivid description of this aspect of affairs in his book *On Not Knowing How to Live.*

> One afternoon I go into the secretarial office to get a chart from the files, and in so doing brush against Sonya. She nods and we pass. A moment later we bump again; for we are reaching into the same drawer and, as it turns out, for the same chart. We smile, she offers it to me, I defer to her, and the incident is over. But in that moment I have noticed her eyes—eloquent, tragic, remote—and something is begun. During the next few days I notice many other things about her, and what is happening to me, I see, is happening also to her. It progresses quickly:

sitting together, holding hands, the sharing of secrets, embracing, and two weeks after the encounter at the filing cabinet we are in a motel outside Hartford, deeply in love, wondering what to do.[1]

He continues to reflect on his experience by expressing his understanding of what happens when he realizes the magic is gone and this affair is over.

We created for each other an illusion. We fell in love, not with each other, but each with the image of himself in the other's eyes. These reflections, flashing back and forth, expanded a modest affection into an overwhelming passion. . . . Such passion feeds on its own hunger, consumes itself. We could not long live on reflected appraisals. There are other things to life, troubles and tasks and preoccupations, and one day, looking at Sonya, I see, not myself, but her concern with other persons, other matters. Failing to find in her that retouched portrait of myself to which I have become so attached, I no longer feel that passionate approval of her which she had so merited. And when next she looks at me she fails to see herself, for I too have other concerns, or else finds an image of herself scaled down from that to which she has become accustomed, whereupon her feeling for me is correspondingly diminished. It was a small thing that got this magic started, and a small thing that made it start to disappear.[2]

It's clear from this account that the overall circumstances of the situation were much more important than the particular person involved. Despite our strong personal feelings about affairs, it's not nearly so personal a matter as we've assumed it to be.

One factor in the role played by the third party is that they are freer to enjoy certain aspects of the relationship that are more difficult when a couple share joint responsibilities and a joint financial base. For instance, one woman who was having an affair with a married man acknowledged how easy it was for her to be happy at her lover's delight in his fancy new sports car. But she recognized that if she had been his wife, she would have reacted just as his wife did, by being upset and critical. She realized that the purchase did not have the financial consequences for her that it did for his wife. And she could see that many of the differences between her and his wife were determined strictly by who was playing what role.

When people are in affairs, they present a side of themselves that's not representative of the whole person. It's a special version of their best aspects, free from the normal responsibilities involved in sharing a total life situation; whereas the roles and structure of family life create many restrictions and responsibilities. A person's affair is not so much a rejection of the mate as a rejection of these role restrictions. This awareness can be especially helpful in dealing with our feelings of comparison with the third party.

Of course, this is much easier to do if the third party is rejected and the marriage survives. But even when a person does choose the third party over their spouse, they frequently learn much later (if the other person takes on the role of spouse) that the specialness had more to do with the earlier role than with the individual person. Many people have an illusion that this new person offers a new life, only to discover after a few years that all the old feelings and issues are there just as in the past. They didn't really change games at all, they only changed the players. Today's third party may be tomorrow's spouse who is unhappy in their marriage.

There's no way to determine how a given person will go about choosing the third party. Of course, most people don't actually *choose* someone; it's not nearly as deliberate and calculated as that would make it seem. The choice is much more a matter of circumstances and exposure than anything else.

WHEN THE THIRD PARTY IS A FRIEND

When the third party turns out to be a personal friend, the pain and anger can be overwhelming. The double blow of being deceived by both a spouse *and* a friend significantly compounds the difficulty of dealing with the situation.

My wife had an affair with a supposed friend of mine. I felt destroyed, I felt dumped on. I wanted to get a gun and kill all of us.

The direction and intensity of the anger seem to be somewhat different according to whether it happens to a man or a woman. While a man may have more *anger* toward a male friend who has an affair with his wife than he has toward his wife, he's likely to place more of the actual *blame* for the affair on her. Even in the midst of being furious with his friend, he usually feels that "men will try to make it with any woman," but his wife shouldn't have given in.

On the other hand, when a woman's husband has an affair with her friend, she is likely to be terribly angry at both of them; but she, too, is likely to blame her friend more than her husband. Both men and women still expect the woman to be the one to prevent an affair. This is because we see the woman as the caretaker of morality in our society, reflecting a continuing (though somewhat diminished) double standard for sexual conduct. Teenage girls still learn that boys will make sexual advances and that it's their responsibility to set the limits on the degree of sexual activity. This leads us to place most of the responsibility for avoiding affairs on the woman; and we usually feel that a woman who doesn't accept this responsibility warrants all the outrage we can muster.

An affair that involves a personal friend is not unusual, but a much more common situation is for the third party to be a social acquaintance. While friendships can usually be severed and contact avoided, acquaintances who happen to move in the same social circles can continue to be a source of irritation, just by virtue of their presence.

This woman is always included in this group of people we still see. I feel very uncomfortable around her and have to hold my tongue to keep from saying nasty things to her.

THE THIRD PARTY AT WORK

Another situation that can be very difficult to deal with is when the third party continues to be a part of the spouse's life through a work connection. One woman reported that she was constantly reminded of the third party's presence in her husband's life because the woman was the receptionist in the large office where he worked.

Every time she called her husband at work, she had to go through this woman in order to speak to him.

This concern about what happens at work has a long history, beginning with the old stereotype of a man having an affair with his secretary (based on a time when a large percentage of the women in the work force were secretaries, many of them young and single). Now that the number of working wives has grown enormously and the variety of jobs has expanded, this has had a significant impact on the number of wives having affairs.

The Redbook Report on Female Sexuality, by Tavris and Sadd, published in 1975, reported on the sex lives of 100,000 married women and showed that 40 percent of them had had an affair by the age of forty. But when the statistics were broken down according to whether or not they were in the workforce, it was found that 33 percent of housewives had an affair by age forty, but 47 percent of full-time employed wives had an affair by age forty. In the intervening years there has been an enormous increase in the number of working women, contributing to the increase in affairs among women. In fact, since opportunity is one of the many factors involved in affairs, the workplace has become the biggest single source of contacts that lead to affairs.

Most of us have seen or felt the attraction that can develop from close working conditions. Almost all of the women with whom James had affairs were women he met through work. And I first became aware of this issue when I was only twenty-five years old and working for a man who was much older, very rich and powerful, quite sophisticated—and who thought I was wonderful. I became enamored of him, and our ongoing close working relationship created a climate where I became seriously tempted to have an affair. This experience convinced me of the vulnerability of *anyone* to an affair; when I saw that I could be tempted, I had to give up my stereotypical thinking about only certain kinds of people becoming involved in affairs.

WHO BECOMES A THIRD PARTY?

Because of our critical attitude toward the third party, we tend to see them in stereotypical terms; we envision them as looking a certain way and acting a certain way. But if we give up the Monogamy Myth and look realistically at the prevalence of affairs, we see that it's impossible to pigeonhole certain types of people who will be third parties. No matter how much we'd like to think otherwise, anyone is susceptible. Part of the reason for the wide range of people who become third parties is because there are differences among people having affairs in the kind of third party they prefer.

As for husbands having affairs, most married men seek out single women as partners. While the primary focus for this choice is on *young,* single women, there's also a specific desire to *avoid* having affairs with women who are married. This thinking is based on not wanting to risk having an irate husband coming after them with violence in mind. But some husbands prefer having affairs with women who are married, feeling that it minimizes the risks in that the women have as much to lose by discovery as they do.

Most wives having affairs choose married partners; they feel safer having an affair with a man who is also married—and therefore more likely to be discreet. However, some wives *don't* choose married men (either because they don't want to hurt another woman or because they prefer the freer, fun-loving lifestyle of single men).

As to the effect of the third party's preferences, in recent years there has been an increase of single career women who prefer at one point in their lives to date married men instead of single ones. Their thinking is based on the fact that they're not interested in a serious involvement that might lead to marriage, and they don't want too many relationship pressures to interfere with the time and energy they need to pursue their careers.

This type of third party is described by Laurel Richardson in her book *The New Other Woman.* Unfortunately, this "new" other woman usually suffers the same kind of disillusionment with her role that the "old" other woman did. While she doesn't mean to become emotionally involved, she usually becomes more dependent on the relationship and less in control of her life than she expected. She often suffers lower self-esteem and eventual rejection when the affair ends. However, the practical issues of the shortage of men and the shortage of time and energy for "having it all" (marriage, family, and career) indicate that this phenomenon is not likely to decrease.

We have very little sympathy for anyone who plays the role of third party; but as a society, we need to stop designating the *good* people and the *bad* people in these situations. We need to realize that everyone involved is a victim of the consequences of our *joint* failure to deal intelligently with this issue.

PART III

· · · · · · ·

THE HEALING PROCESS

5

· · · · · · ·

Rebuilding Self-esteem

The devastation felt by a person who learns of their partner's affair is greater than many of us can imagine. Often, it's more than just a reaction to that particular event; it's also a reaction to the loss of the dream they had for their marriage and for how their lives should work out. While it's difficult for a person in this situation to deal with the pain and sense of loss they feel, it's even more difficult for them to deal with the damage to their pride and self-esteem.

Unfortunately, most of us have a difficult time maintaining our self-esteem even in normal times, so a partner's affair compounds our natural tendency to put ourselves down for anything we view as a shortcoming. Most people focus far more of their attention on their mistakes than on their achievements. For instance, if we have ten tasks to accomplish and succeed with nine of them, it's the one failure we're likely to dwell on. This preoccupation with our faults can block our awareness of our positive qualities and cause us to be unnecessarily hard on ourselves.

I've seen this demonstrated repeatedly in workshops I've conducted on personal growth and self-esteem. In one exercise (which is called a "bragging" session), each person is asked to list all their positive traits or abilities. Some people can't seem to get started, as if they can't think of anything positive about themselves. Others make a very short list and have a great deal of trouble adding to it. (Oddly enough, making a list of their weaknesses is relatively easy for most people.)

The next step in this exercise is reading the lists aloud to the group. Since this can feel awkward and embarrassing, the group is instructed to give verbal reinforcement as each list is read (saying things like "right on," "yes, sir," "that's true," "tell us some more") and to clap whenever they feel like it. Even with this encouragement, most people feel very uncomfortable "bragging" about themselves in this way. While this is a training exercise in a contrived setting, it provides insight into the depth of our problems with self-esteem.

ASSESSING THE DAMAGE
· · · · · · ·

There is no simple exercise for rebuilding self-esteem following a mate's affair. In fact, we can't appreciate the difficulty of the task without a much clearer understanding of just how extensive the damage can be. One way of getting a better sense of the extent of the damage is to focus on the words people use in trying to express their feelings about their mates' affairs; they feel devastated, deceived, humiliated, and filled with shame.

DEVASTATION

This is the most frequently used word by people trying to describe their feelings when they learn of their partner's affair. This may be because it's the first of the many emotions they encounter with this experience. The basis for this sense of devastation is the shock of facing the truth (especially if a person has not suspected or has denied their suspicions). But even if there has been a strong suspicion of an affair, they still experience the full force of the emotional impact when they find out for sure. This period is usually the most physically draining, making a person feel sick, lifeless, and helpless. It has the power to temporarily destroy their self-esteem.

DECEPTION

For many people, the deception and dishonesty involved causes even more pain than the fact that their spouse had sex with someone else. This is a very private kind of pain, reflecting a deep disappointment in their mate and in the relationship. Things aren't what they seemed and the spouse isn't the person they pretended to be. Some people feel intense anger, even rage. Others feel a deep sense of hurt, of being wounded. While not always the case, the reaction often reflects the degree of damage to a person's self-esteem. For instance, a person who says, "How *could* you," may suffer more damage to their self-esteem than a person who says, "How *dare* you."

HUMILIATION

After getting beyond the immediate devastation and the pain of being deceived, the person whose partner has had an affair is likely to feel humiliated that others know about it (and may have known it all along). For most people, this feels like a public loss of respect. Their embarrassment may cause them to avoid public groups and public gatherings because they think everyone will be whispering about them. And it causes many people to hide from everyone while they try to regain some of their self-esteem.

SHAME

This goes beyond humiliation in that it assumes more than just the self-consciousness of others knowing about the affair; it includes feeling that others are judging them as responsible for it. Since affairs are seen as "improper" and "dishonorable," a person whose partner has an affair feels tainted by the situation and ashamed of the fact that it happened. They may be overwhelmed with feelings of remorse and regret for having married someone who would have an affair, further damaging their self-esteem.

SUICIDE AND SELF-DESTRUCTION

The emotions involved in dealing with a partner's affair can become so overwhelming and a person's self-esteem can be so badly damaged that it threatens their physical and mental well-being. This experience has led some people to turn to alcohol or drugs and others to have a nervous breakdown or be in need of professional attention. It has also led to considerations of suicide. While some only contemplate suicide, others actually attempt it. This is the ultimate self-rejection, demonstrating a total loss of self-esteem.

In order to comprehend this level of desperation on the part of the person who learns of their partner's affair, we need to understand the relationship between suicide and self-esteem. I first became aware of this connection during the 70s when I was conducting workshops in life/career planning. In an exercise aimed at clarifying values, people were asked to rank the worst thing that could happen to them. The list included going blind, losing a limb, having a complete nervous breakdown, losing all their friends, and undergoing complete financial bankruptcy.

Invariably, the choice of most people most of the time was that the worst of these events was "going blind." However, few people who go blind resort to suicide, whereas many people have committed suicide over bankruptcy. This can be explained in terms of the meaning attached to the two: Bankruptcy is seen as a personal failure, whereas blindness is assumed to be beyond personal control. Since the reaction to an event is likely to be determined by how much a person feels responsible for what happened, it's no wonder the issue of affairs has been so damaging to the self-esteem of those who face it. This sense of responsibility is based on the tendency for a person to blame themselves when their partner has an affair (either because they feel personally inadequate or because they chose a man or woman who deceived them in this way).

While the overall impact is equally destructive to men and to women whose partners have had affairs, there may be some subtle differences in their thinking when this happens.

Men have to struggle with the idea that it's somehow worse for a man to have an unfaithful wife than for a woman to have an unfaithful husband. This attitude is based on a couple of outdated beliefs. First, wives were once seen as the property of their husbands and men were expected to "keep their wives in line." It was a blemish on their manhood if they failed to maintain this control. Second, there's a longstanding interpretation of men having affairs as a case of "boys will be boys," somewhat lessening the personal stigma attached to having a husband who falls into this category. But there's no such rationalization applied to women having affairs, leaving husbands with no way to depersonalize the situation, either in their own eyes or in the eyes of others.

For women, the damage to their self-esteem from a partner's affair is compounded by the fact that relationships hold a higher priority in the lives of most women. While men have identified themselves primarily in terms of their success in work or other endeavors, women still (despite recent strides in equality) tend to identify very strongly with the success of their primary relationship. So a woman who feels she has "failed" in her relationship is likely to feel a severe overall sense of failure, causing enormous damage to her self-esteem.

CHANGING OUR WAY OF THINKING
• • • • • • •

Any effort to address the issue of rebuilding self-esteem must begin with changing our way of interpreting affairs as a personal failure. The most destructive aspect of our belief in the Monogamy Myth is the damage to a person's self-esteem caused by seeing affairs only as an individual problem. As discussed earlier, we need to replace this purely personal view of affairs with an understanding of the societal context within which they take place. This new understanding is essential for a person to successfully deal with the pain of their partner's affair. And it's essential that they deal with this pain before trying to build a positive self-image. This includes accepting the fact that the affair happened, overcoming personal blame, and overcoming the secrecy that surrounds affairs.

ACCEPTING THE FACT THAT THE AFFAIR HAPPENED

The longer a person denies the reality of what has happened, the longer they delay the healing process. Of course, at some point everyone has to acknowledge that the affair happened, but that's not the same as accepting it. Acceptance doesn't mean liking it; acceptance means reaching a degree of understanding, of making peace with the fact that it happened. This is one of the goals of this book—to help people gain some perspective on affairs so they can reach this stage of acceptance in order to recover from their experience.

The depth of the emotions and the initial devastation upon learning of a mate's affair do not mean a person can't reach this point of accepting what has happened. Of course, it takes time and a lot of hard work, but it can be done. The critical ingredient in being able to accept the reality of the situation is rejecting the Monogamy Myth and working to overcome the emotional reaction with a more rational understanding. Here's a look at one man's struggle to get to this point.

> *When she walked out two years ago, I really wanted to kill myself. Well, I've got my head on straight now, I hope. I still wish it hadn't happened, but "if only" is a waste of time.*

This illustrates the idea behind acceptance, that it's not necessary to like what happened or to agree with what happened; it's only necessary to *accept* that it happened and that nothing is going to change that fact. This allows a person to go on with their lives, because they don't try to pretend it didn't happen. They are then able to let go of the past and begin focusing on the future. Here's the way one woman described the change in her feelings when she finally arrived at this stage of acceptance.

> *It feels so good to* not *be jealous and bitter anymore! (Is this the same woman who slashed tires on her husband's truck and pounded in a fender with a hammer?)*

OVERCOMING PERSONAL BLAME

As discussed in the first chapter, our tendency to feel personal blame for our mate's affair is the most critical factor in making it so difficult to overcome. We need to remind ourselves, over and over, of a few basic principles: "Do not take it personally. You did not personally cause it. You could not have personally prevented it." And just as important: "Your spouse is not totally to blame. There are many factors in society as a whole that contribute to affairs, actually making it difficult to *avoid* having an affair."

This change in thinking is not as difficult as it might first appear, since our reaction to any event is based on how we interpret it. And our way of interpreting an event is not inherent or automatic; it's learned. If we learn to explain something in a personal way, we can unlearn it. We can change our interpretation of an event by applying a more rational understanding of it.

I clearly remember how it felt when I went through the process of shifting my thinking about personal blame. I kept asking, "Where did I fail?" When James tried to tell me it had "nothing to do with me," I said it had *everything* to do with me. When he said that I "shouldn't take it personally," I said that was the only way I *could* take it. As I got more information about other marriages in which affairs had taken place, I finally came to see that his having affairs didn't depend on what I did or didn't do. Anyone is vulnerable to their partner's having an affair, regardless of how good a mate they may be.

To finally accept that the affair was not their fault is one of the biggest steps for a person who has had their self-esteem shattered by their partner's affair. They are able to feel much better about themselves when they stop seeing the problem as totally due to their "failures." Overcoming this personal view of affairs also makes it possible for them to take the next important step in their recovery, overcoming their secrecy about what has happened.

OVERCOMING THE SECRECY ABOUT AFFAIRS

One reason it has taken so long for society to recognize the seriousness of this problem is because of the way most people keep their pain hidden, if at all possible. Some people become obsessed with the idea of keeping their experience secret from others. One man said this was his most pressing concern; that, in fact, he had become almost paranoid about other people "knowing."

The process of keeping this information from others increases the feelings of shame and embarrassment (because if it weren't seen as shameful, it wouldn't need to be kept secret). And the longer it's kept secret, the stronger the feelings of shame. So the secrecy and the problem with self-esteem serve to reinforce each other. It's hard to talk openly when you take it personally, and it's hard not to take it personally if you are closed off from outside sources that could help in getting beyond the strictly personal interpretation. An important factor in rebuilding self-esteem is breaking this cycle of secrecy and isolation. The first step is to honestly discuss this situation with just one other person and talk to them about your feelings.

Talking with Others

Traditionally, men have been conditioned to hide their feelings, so when a man faces the fact that his partner has had an affair, it's not surprising that he doesn't talk about it. And even though women have typically been able to talk about their feelings, in this case most women try to keep them hidden as well. For both men and women, much of the pain and frustration of dealing with affairs is directly linked to this effort to deal with their fears while hiding their feelings from the outside world.

A person needs to be able to talk about what has happened in order to recover a sense of equilibrium after discovering their partner's affair. When they try to deal with it alone, they often become even more frustrated and confused.

> *I haven't told anyone about it. The situation is tearing me apart, and I don't know what to do about it or who to turn to, and I feel so alone so much of the time.*

As discussed earlier, the isolation suffered by people in this situation is often motivated by their desire to avoid the sympathy and pity of others. This was the case with me, at least in the beginning. When I began to suspect my husband was having affairs, I tried to hide it—from friends, from family, from everybody! I didn't want other people to see me as pitiful or feel sorry for me.

Unfortunately, this has been an understandable fear. The general reaction in society as a whole *has* been to feel sorry for people in this situation, or to see it as a reflection on them personally. There's a tendency to think they've failed to be all they should have been to prevent it, or at the very least that they should have known it was happening and done something about it (usually meaning either giving an ultimatum or getting a divorce). It will continue to be difficult for people to talk openly about their experience with affairs as long as we as a society are so judgmental and limited in our own understanding.

This habit of hiding our personal problems is slowly changing as we recognize that most of our problems are shared by others who are also putting on a front. It becomes much easier to admit a problem when society recognizes that the individuals dealing with the problem are not personally to blame for it. We've seen the benefit of this kind of understanding in a number of other areas, most visibly that of being an alcoholic (or the adult child of an alcoholic) or a victim of incest or physical abuse.

Of course, it's easier to talk to someone who has had personal experience in dealing with affairs, but this is not essential. On the other hand, it's not reasonable to talk to just anybody, because there's likely to be a wide range of reactions from various friends or family members. It's important to find someone who can suspend judgment and participate in a discussion of affairs beyond the strictly personal view. It's also important to avoid talking to a person who will reinforce the feelings of embarrassment or shame. Receiving outward encouragement from a person who secretly feels pity or criticism is likely to be detected by the person who is already struggling with feelings of personal blame or inadequacy. And this kind of patronizing attitude will cause even more damage to their self-esteem.

The reason it's so important for people struggling with affairs to talk to a person who can be truly supportive is because the point is not simply to talk, but to process the feelings in such a way as to make the situation feel a little bit different, a little more manageable. Since this is a very complex problem, the process of talking about it has to be done over and over. It takes many sessions of talking with different people in order to move the process along.

SELF-ESTEEM AND THE SPOUSE
· · · · · · ·

A factor that often affects a person's efforts to rebuild their self-esteem is the attitude of the spouse who had an affair. We've seen how desperately most people want to know more about what happened in their own situation—and how resistant most spouses are to tell them any details. But sometimes a person is willing to talk, which can lead to a much better understanding.

I could ask any question I wanted about the affair and it was answered without hiding anything. We are still happily married. And I think we have both grown from what has happened.

While talking doesn't guarantee this kind of happy ending, it was clear from the reports of the members of BAN that honest communication plays a significant role in a couple's ability to come to grips with the issues they face and to rebuild their marriage. Also, it's somewhat easier to rebuild self-esteem if the marriage continues, because the failure of the marriage sometimes adds to the feelings of personal failure. One woman (who put forth a great deal of effort to save her "apparently hopeless marriage") felt that failing to save the marriage was even more damaging to her sense of self-worth than the affair itself.

Problems with self-esteem are not restricted to the person who discovers their partner's affair. Usually the person who had an affair also has a difficult time rebuilding self-esteem. In fact, sometimes their feelings of guilt make it impossible for them to stay in the relationship.

Her guilt is so great that she can't stay with me. I want to work it out, but she can't forgive herself for what she's done.

The person who has been hurt by their partner's affair may find it difficult to have any sympathy for their partner's feelings at this time. But it will work for the benefit of both parties if there can be some compassion for the pain that each of them may be suffering. Even if there's some immediate gratification in punishing the person who had an affair, it doesn't provide any long-term satisfaction—and it certainly doesn't contribute anything to the prospects for saving the marriage.

Unfortunately, it's not unusual for the person who had an affair to deal with their own issues of guilt or embarrassment by blocking out the impact of their behavior on their mate. They may not be conscious of the effect of this kind of reaction, but it often leaves the mate feeling their partner doesn't *care* about their pain.

When a person feels they can't get through to the partner who had an affair, this further diminishes their sense of self-worth. As a result, they may become preoccupied with finding out just what their partner thinks of them and desperate to impress them as a way of rebuilding their self-esteem.

This situation often creates a strange irony: A person is *less* likely to get what they want from someone when they want it so desperately. They're much more likely to get the recognition they want from their partner if they recognize their own worth and have a healthy self-image. They need to reach the point of disassociating their self-worth from the actions or attitudes of others. It's important that they strive to feel good about themselves and not be dependent upon any other person for their self-esteem.

ALLOWING TIME TO HEAL
· · · · · · ·

Most people aren't prepared for just how long it takes to recover from the experience of a mate's affair and to reach a point of personal healing. They get tired; they get discouraged; they start feeling the time will never come when they can have peace and love in their hearts instead of bitterness and pain. They begin to wonder if they'll ever get to the point where the memories (and the emotions they generate) are no longer a problem.

All too often, when people finally feel they're doing better in coping with their feelings, they get knocked down again by some memory that comes back and interferes with whatever is currently happening.

I'll feel okay. Then something will happen—a mixed message, a threatening communication, a song, and all the pain will flood back into me and I feel alone.

Learning to cope with a spouse's affair is so like a cancer. At times it seems to be arrested, but then it reoccurs and the pain starts all over again.

We want to get beyond this, and most of the time I am able to do just that, and then something from the past ten years will trigger me and there is this overwhelming hurt or another question.

The frustration of not being able to avoid these reminders of a mate's affair is common among those who stay married, especially if they feel they have weathered the storm and arrived at a new and better place in the relationship. But this can also be a problem for those who get divorced and are trying to move on to other areas of focus in their lives.

It's important to the healing process that a person recognize that personal recovery from the emotional impact of this experience is not determined by whether or not the relationship survives. Dealing with the marriage/divorce dilemma is a completely separate issue, one that will be examined more carefully in a later chapter.

Some people who stay married make a good personal recovery, overcoming the emotional damage and renewing their commitment to the relationship. But many others who stay married never recover emotionally. They spend the rest of their lives bitter and resentful, and the relationship remains strained and distant. The same is true for those who get out of the relationship. Some make a good recovery and go on to form a more satisfying relationship with someone else. And some never recover, carrying the emotional burden with them into whatever relationships they have in the future—or perhaps even avoiding any future involvements.

Regardless of whether a person chooses to stay married or get a divorce, it's essential that they be patient with the amount of time it takes to heal from a partner's affair. It's also important to keep in mind that time alone won't bring about healing. Healing results from the way the time is used. For instance, I remember my frustration at continuing to have painful thoughts about James's affairs long after I wanted to forget about them. It sometimes seemed that the harder I tried to forget, the more the memories would cling. I used to wish for amnesia. There seemed no other way to absolutely forget.

I finally came to see that it's not a matter of being able to stop thinking; it's a matter of changing the *way* we think. Any effort to avoid thinking about the affairs before they're fully dealt with is a losing proposition. Disturbing thoughts are likely to continue as long as the issue is not completely resolved in a person's own mind. The only question is whether the thoughts will be voluntary or involuntary.

DELIBERATELY FOCUSING ON THE PROBLEM
• • • • • • •

At first sight it might seem unreasonable to voluntarily focus on thoughts that are disturbing. But when they are suppressed and held inside, they may surface at any time, without warning. When painful thoughts involuntarily come to mind, a person is not prepared or able to deal with the feelings. So the main reason to continue the effort to deal with this issue is that trying to avoid dealing with it doesn't mean avoiding the pain. It just means risking that the pain may never go away.

After two years I still find myself getting upset and depressed when the affair comes to my mind. I don't try to think about it or dwell on the fact, but somehow it keeps popping up.

There's a significant advantage to being deliberate in thinking through the issues related to affairs. First of all, voluntarily focusing on the problem makes it easier to talk about the experience without the kind of pain that comes from unexpectedly being caught up in disturbing thoughts. It becomes much easier to deal with it when there's some measure of control over when and how the thinking takes place.

Also, if a person tries to avoid thinking about the affair, there's a tendency to try to pretend it never happened. And this avoidance of reality interferes with a person's ability to deal with life in a meaningful way. This issue has to be faced head-on in order to take the edge off the pain and get it outside, not tucked away on the inside where it never gets better.

BELIEVING IT'S POSSIBLE TO RECOVER
· · · · · · ·

Unfortunately, some people believe there's no hope for overcoming the pain of their partner's affair, regardless of whether or not they talk about it. But the first step to recovery is believing it's possible. I know from my own experience that it *is* possible to recover from a mate's affair. I understand how it feels in the beginning when you're overwhelmed with fear and pain. When I first became suspicious that James was having affairs, I didn't think I'd be able to survive if it were true. My emotions were very much in control with almost no perspective to offset them. I honestly felt at that time that my life was ruined.

I gradually came to realize that I wasn't alone, either in my experience or in my personal interpretation of it. As my understanding of affairs grew stronger, my self-esteem grew stronger as well. It felt a little like a seesaw, as I gradually shifted from being controlled by my emotions to being able to rationally understand what had happened.

This process involved years of talking about my experience with a great many people and reading everything I could find about the subject of affairs. Gradually, its grip on me loosened and then slipped away one day when I didn't even notice. There was no great moment of truth when I knew I was over the hump. It was a very slow process of turning it inside out and upside down until I had control of it instead of it having control over me.

This is a common dilemma for many people—getting enough understanding to overpower their emotions. Often they are able to accept and understand what has happened intellectually long before they recover emotionally. One person talked about sounding very reasonable and rational on the outside while dying inside from feelings of hurt and anger.

I can honestly say that I never get emotionally stirred up and upset anymore about my husband's affairs, and I don't think I could have reached this point without deliberately talking about and dealing with the issue. I don't think I'm unique. I'm no more forgiving or understanding or strong or unemotional than anyone else. But I licked these emotions, and I believe anyone can. In fact, not only is it possible for a person to recover from this experience, but it's also possible for them to come out of it with a greater sense of self-worth than before it happened.

I have reconciled events and I have healed. I've learned to see myself in a much softer light than before. I feel very strong and capable, and this has brought a new kind of security to my life. I have learned from my experiences, and I value the idea that where I stand is only a result of the journey that brought me here.

Part of the potential payoff for a person who successfully deals with the issue of affairs is the possibility of redefining the way they see themselves and their place in the world. Those who succeed in doing this are those who accept that they are now different because of their experience, but recognize that they are okay. While none of us would choose this as a way of achieving personal growth, it is nevertheless possible for that to be the result.

6

· · · · · · ·

Trust, Honesty, and Communication

Trust may have been taken for granted prior to the crisis of dealing with affairs. But people who previously assumed their relationship would be monogamous come to realize that trust needs to be based on honesty and honest communication, not on blind faith. These three factors (trust, honesty, and communication) are like the legs of a three-legged stool, each depending on the other to provide the stability that's needed for a solid relationship. It's unfortunate that more relationships aren't based on this understanding from the beginning, since it's much more difficult to regain trust after it has been broken.

> *I'm not sure I'll ever trust him again—or really love him. And I do believe you can't have a real marriage without trust and love.*

REBUILDING TRUST
· · · · · · ·

If the person who had an affair is willing to answer questions about what happened, this can go a long way toward rebuilding trust. We've seen how difficult this is for most people to do; but unanswered questions become a barrier, making certain a couple will never be as close as they'd like. Many people feel they can never trust their mate again if their mate refuses to answer their questions. "How can I trust that they will be honest in the future if they won't be honest about the past?" This was a significant part of my ability to trust James after he told me about his affairs. In fact, his honesty provided a basis for my trust that hadn't existed before. His willingness to answer all my questions caused me to trust him more than I had trusted him before the affairs ever happened.

Another important factor in rebuilding trust is what a person *does*, not just what they say. For instance, one man who had had an affair tried to pacify his partner by saying, "You don't have anything to worry about now." But he didn't let her know when he'd be home or where he'd been when he did get home. So while his words said, "Trust me," his actions gave her plenty of reason *not* to trust him.

Sometimes a single event can lead to a tremendous increase in feelings of trust and confidence. One man (whose trust had been completely shattered by his wife's affair) told of an incident that happened about six months after her affair ended. She was contacted by the guy she had had the affair with, who was hoping they might resume their relationship now that things had quieted down. She told the man not to contact her again, that she was totally committed to her husband and their marriage. And, more important, she told her husband of the conversation. For her husband, this was confirmation for having placed his trust in her again.

For most people, rebuilding trust is not a smooth process. There may be periods of improvement or times when the trust seems to be stronger, only to find doubts returning once again.

> *I am doing much better than I was a year ago at this time, and most of the time feel that we are going to make it, but I still have my moments of total doubt about us or anything.*

> *Although my trust has strengthened, I don't know if it will ever reach preaffair levels.*

Much of the hesitancy people feel about trusting again after having been deceived is that they often feel they were naive to have trusted in the first place, and they don't want to repeat the same mistake. This concern is warranted to the extent that their earlier trust probably was based on their belief in the Monogamy Myth, assuming they would never have to deal with this issue.

Developing trust depends on facing the reality that the issue of affairs is one that every couple needs to address and making a point of knowing your partner's beliefs and attitudes about monogamy instead of silently wondering how they feel. For instance, James is honest in acknowledging that he finds other women attractive and desirable, and we are able to talk about how he feels about the fact that he's not acting on those attractions. Our honest discussion of this issue allows me to feel I really know him, making it easier to trust him.

Many people struggle with the question of whether it's reasonable to trust again after their partner has had an affair. The somewhat ambiguous answer is, "It depends." It depends on whether they know where they stand with their mate and know what's going on between them. It depends on whether they share their thoughts and feelings on an ongoing basis, or whether they mostly have to guess about what the other person is thinking and feeling.

The only way to avoid guessing about the facts is to know the facts. This "knowing the facts," however, may not be as comforting and reassuring as one might hope. Granted, it will combat the suspicion; but there's no way to avoid all discomfort. It's a matter of choosing which course of action brings the most peace of mind.

For instance, one woman was having a difficult time dealing with her suspicions that her husband was attracted to a particular woman in their social circle. They had discussed these issues in general and had agreed that they wouldn't volunteer this kind of information but, if asked, they would answer each other's questions honestly. When she finally got up enough nerve to ask him about her suspicions, he acknowledged that he was aware of a growing attraction to this woman, but had not been tempted to act on it. While she felt some anxiety at hearing this, she also felt good about her decision to ask. His talking so openly about his feelings diminished her concern that he might be tempted to withhold this kind of information, reinforcing her sense of trust in their commitment to honesty.

So a person can actively deal with their suspicions, but it's not by embracing the fairy-tale notion of their spouse never finding another person attractive. It's by acknowledging that their spouse is likely to be attracted to others, but not having to guess as to what they might do about the attraction.

The benefit of talking about this particular issue goes beyond just getting information, however. The process of discussing the attractions actually decreases the likelihood of acting on them, because it focuses on the potential problems of acting on them, whereas when a person is tempted to have an affair, their private thoughts usually dwell only on the potential pleasures. There's an added fascination and excitement about feelings that are kept secret as compared to those that are acknowledged and discussed. Shedding the cold light of day on secret desires goes a long way toward diminishing their power.

This process of acknowledging attractions and discussing how they are to be handled is one that both married and unmarried couples need to address *prior to any problem* with outside affairs. Constantly wondering and worrying about this issue creates a strain between partners that may prevent their developing a sense of confidence in each other. They need to talk through their feelings about monogamy and attractions to other people on an ongoing basis as their relationship develops.

Of course, this is another instance where societal factors play an important role. Since open discussion of these issues contradicts the general code of secrecy, it makes it more difficult for couples to do the talking necessary to establish trust. And since the Monogamy Myth perpetuates the erroneous belief that couples who are "in love" and committed to each other won't have affairs, it discourages the communication about this issue that is so essential. Most people would prefer to be able to get this settled once and for all. But dealing with the issue of monogamy is an ongoing process, not something that can be established on the basis of one discussion or one promise.

DON'T TRUST A PROMISE OF MONOGAMY
· · · · · · ·

Most people feel that rebuilding trust in a partner who had an affair depends on their mate promising to be monogamous in the future. It's understandable that they want some kind of reassurance, but a promise of monogamy is no guarantee (as is clear from the fact that this promise is assumed to be part of the wedding vows, which have already been broken).

In the case of one couple (who had spent about six months dealing with the fallout from his affair), a decision was made to stay together and have a ceremony to renew their wedding vows in front of friends and family. The first time they had simply assumed monogamy, but this time they were making a clear commitment to be monogamous. She felt sure she could trust his promise of monogamy; so she put the past behind, thinking affairs would never again be an issue she need be concerned about.

Unfortunately, this issue was not over, as she soon learned. A few months after the renewal of their marriage vows, she got a call from an anonymous "friend" who informed her that her husband was still seeing the woman he had had the affair with and that he was with her at that time. At first, his wife didn't believe it; but she couldn't resist going to verify it for herself. When she found him with the other woman, she went berserk. She screamed at her husband and physically attacked the other woman. She was overcome with rage and hatred, for them as well as for herself for being duped by his renewed promise of monogamy.

He finally admitted he had never ended the affair as he had said, but promised to do so now. But it was too late; at that point, she was unwilling to hear anything he had to say. She felt there was no way she could ever believe him again. The pain and embarrassment of renewing their commitment publicly (when, in fact, she was the only one who meant it) was more than she could bear. She filed for divorce shortly thereafter.

Monogamy doesn't depend on a one-time decision, whether it's made at the beginning of a relationship or following an affair. Even if a person intends to be monogamous when they make that commitment, it doesn't mean they won't change their thinking at some future time. When there's only a promise of monogamy, there's no way to determine when a person's thinking is changing and they are moving toward the possibility of an affair.

If there's no security in a promise of monogamy, this still leaves the problem of finding a way to overcome the fears and doubts that most people feel after dealing with a partner's affair. (It's important to note that trust is likely to be a problem not only if the marriage continues, but also in any new relationship that develops in the future.)

A COMMITMENT TO HONESTY
· · · · · · ·

The way to rebuild trust is not by making a promise of monogamy, but by making a commitment to honesty. There's a tendency to think of honesty only as telling something that was previously kept secret. But the main power of honesty is in sharing *feelings*. When a couple share their deepest feelings about everything, including the "scary" stuff (like attractions to other people or fears of their partner having an affair), they develop a deeper understanding of each other. Many people think that talking about such emotional issues will inevitably cause problems. But it's far more likely that it will lead to a closer relationship because of the comfort involved in feeling you will be told the truth about anything that comes up.

It's ironic that while honesty is recognized as important to a relationship, most people also fear it and see it as a risk to the security of the relationship. Unfortunately, they fail to see the risk involved with *dishonesty*. Part of the reason for the current fear of honesty is because of the kind of honesty that became prevalent in the 60s with "saying it like it is" and "letting it all hang out." This led many people to see honesty as thoughtlessly hurting each other with bluntness; which, in turn, led to excusing dishonesty as tact and kindness toward others. This is a narrow, shortsighted view of honesty and a naive view of dishonesty.

Of course, honesty can be harmful if it's practiced with no regard for its impact on the other person. But there's much more involved than simply deciding *whether* to be honest. It's important to focus on *when*, *why*, and *how*—paying attention to timing, motivation, and caring. These factors will be discussed more thoroughly in the guidelines for developing good communication later in this chapter.

The fear of being hurt is one of the main drawbacks to a whole-hearted pursuit of honesty. Because of this fear, many people question just how much honesty is good or desirable in an intimate relationship. They rationalize that they're being honest as long as they're not actively lying. But honesty is much more than simply not lying; it's not *withholding* information or feelings that are important to the relationship. The idea of this kind of "total" honesty seems so unrealistic and unachievable for most people that they may feel there's no point in even trying to be honest. But developing honesty is a process, not an event. And the goal for each couple (which is certainly attainable) is to gradually increase their *level* of honesty.

It's understandable that there will be feelings of anxiety associated with trying to establish a relationship based on open, honest communication. Lack of honesty tends to break down relationships over the years, and it becomes very difficult to change old ways of relating. The effort to convince a spouse to be honest (who is obviously resisting the effort) becomes a very trying experience, especially when dealing with an emotional issue like affairs.

One woman described how her husband had ignored all her efforts to talk about his affairs—he just wanted to forget the whole thing and expected her to do the same. She was extremely frustrated that he thought she should just accept him back without working through her feelings about what had happened. She felt unable to stay with him without more honesty, so she eventually left the relationship.

Sometimes when a person can't get their partner to talk, they begin to wonder if they would have been better off never knowing about the affair. I understand this way of thinking; I still wish it had never happened to me. But since it *did* happen, I don't wish I'd never found out about it. My strength and vitality as a person come from knowing what's going on in my world, not from pretending that what I don't know won't hurt me. That attitude only robs a person of the right to lead their life based on the facts instead of on pretense. It's important to believe you're a person worthy of honesty and to insist on a relationship that reflects that worth.

Honesty was the motivator for my husband telling me about his affairs. He became uncomfortable with deceiving me and felt I deserved more fairness and equality in the relationship. We also relied on honesty as a way of working through all the feelings that had built up over the years. And honesty was the basis of our commitment to the kind of relationship we wanted to develop in the future. While I wanted a monogamous relationship, I recognized the fallacy of a promise of monogamy. So James didn't promise to be monogamous; he promised to be honest. But the result of our commitment to honesty has led to our being monogamous during the fifteen years since that commitment was made.

Our honesty is not restricted to issues related to affairs; we're honest about everything relevant to our relationship. This includes talking about our personal hopes and dreams as well as our private fears and anxieties. While this kind of honesty brings a special bond to a relationship, there's a personal benefit as well that is often overlooked. Honesty provides a firm place to stand in the world. It forms a solid basis from which to embark upon the challenges of everyday life. It provides strength in dealing with the many issues everyone faces outside their relationship. Many people report that developing an honest relationship with their spouse helped them to communicate more honestly in *all* their relationships.

REINFORCING HONESTY

The ability to succeed in dealing honestly with an affair does not depend solely on the attitude and behavior of the one who had the affair. Their partner's reaction is critical because it serves either to reinforce honesty or to discourage it. Honesty about affairs comes in stages. First, there is the admission that it happened, then the many details that contribute to seeing the whole picture. A partner's reaction to the initial fact of the affair has a lot to do with the willingness of the person who had an affair to share any of the details.

A person who discovers their mate's affair usually feels justified in venting their feelings of hurt and anger. While they certainly have a right to those feelings, they need to recognize that punishing their mate for telling the truth will almost surely put an end to any further honesty. So while it may seem *unfair,* it's in their own best interest to try to reinforce whatever honesty is received if there is to be much hope for the honesty continuing.

Supporting a partner's honesty often takes enormous patience. One man said he felt his effort to get his wife to open up and talk was like peeling an onion, with each skin coming off with great difficulty. He continued to encourage her and to show his appreciation for her efforts to be honest, so she finally became convinced it was safe to tell him the truth. It took a long time, but they were able to stay together and develop a relationship that was closer than it had been prior to the affair.

In another case, a man told of the terrible price his wife paid for being honest with him about her affair. By his own admission, he lashed out at her to try to hurt her back. She decided she had made a mistake by being honest about her affair and became afraid to tell him anything else. But she hung in without trying to defend herself against his constant barrage of criticism. Finally, he came to realize that she must love him very much to tolerate all he had put her through. He felt thankful she hadn't left, and began trying to make up for the damage that had been done.

This can be quite a challenge for the person who asks for honesty—to avoid punishing their partner for telling them what they want to know. It's understandable that a person feels bad about some of the information they receive, but this can be balanced by feeling good about their partner's honesty. This was my experience, feeling so positive about James's honesty in answering everything I asked him that it diminished the pain of what he had to say. This kind of honest communication is important, not only in dealing with what has happened, but in determining the nature of the relationship in the future.

DEVELOPING HONEST COMMUNICATION
· · · · · · ·

Communication is much more than simply opening your mouth and letting words come out. Developing the ability to talk honestly with your partner is a complicated process. There are six factors that are important to a successful effort to develop honest communication:

- motive: being motivated by a desire to improve the relationship
- timing: considering the best time to have a conversation
- location: choosing surroundings that support communication

- attitude: having an attitude conducive to a productive discussion
- responsiveness: listening in such a way as to encourage honesty
- expectations: openness to whatever results from this effort

MOTIVE

The success of any effort to establish a pattern of honest communication depends on the motivation behind it. It's critical that you pursue this goal because you want to develop closeness and intimacy, not because you want to take advantage of the other person. You must want to develop trust, which calls for resisting any impulse to use your partner's honesty as a way of catching them in a mistake and punishing them for it. You must be committed to sharing yourself and to being known by your partner, not just using your honesty as a way to unburden and blame all your problems on them.

It's important that you want to find out what your partner really feels and that you not deny them the right to feel that way. You must want to share your thoughts and feelings for the purpose of being understood, not in order to justify everything you do. You must be interested in exchanging information about all kinds of subjects to reach a better understanding, rather than debating certain issues just to prove you're right. You must have a desire to find solutions for problems instead of simply complaining about them.

TIMING

Since there's no ideal time to begin this process of developing honest communication, it's important not to wait until it just happens. It's good to plan a time to talk, and to protect that time. But you need not always plan it. Too many "scheduled" talks can increase the tension in anticipating them.

Sometimes you may feel a special need to talk, and it's important that you tell your partner instead of expecting them to read your mind. Of course, you need to be sensitive to your partner's receptivity for a talk. The benefit of the experience depends on *both* people being in a position to give it their full attention. (If your partner is never receptive, then it's an entirely different problem and indicates an uphill battle in developing good communication—or a good relationship.)

If your partner never wants to talk, honestly ask yourself if your attitude is overwhelmingly critical. No time will be a good time if you use the talks only to criticize your partner. Men particularly have come to fear that "a talk" means a session of being criticized, understandably causing them to resist when they suspect this is the purpose of the request.

You need to communicate frequently and not wait for things to build up to a marathon session. Also, be sure to talk at a time when you're not distracted by television or the presence of other people. And most important, use prime time for talking. Don't wait for the last thing at night when you're tired. This is a priority activity that needs and deserves your best energy.

LOCATION

Some people like to have a particular place for regularly scheduled discussions. However, it's also important to incorporate the talks into your regular routine and not see them as a completely separate activity, isolated from life as a whole. It can be stimulating to vary the location for talking instead of always choosing the same spot. (People sometimes get in ruts, sitting in the same place and saying the same things.)

Of course, it needs to be a place where both of you feel comfortable. This doesn't mean it should never be in a public place; but if a public place is chosen, be sure this was not a ploy to prevent any possibility of expressing emotions.

For especially heavy conversations, talking outdoors (weather permitting) can bring a certain calmness and peacefulness that can help diminish the tension. I personally remember the positive effect of the hours we spent walking on the beach and talking during the day following the night James told me about his affairs. It was very therapeutic.

Whatever the location, stay physically close together while talking—close enough to touch, if not actually touching. You're less likely to speak loudly or harshly if you're close together instead of talking across the room.

ATTITUDE

The most critical attitude for approaching your intimate conversations is one of honesty. This doesn't mean being 100 percent honest about every thought that goes through your mind. That would be an impossible task anyway. It means talking about any thought that has an effect on the quality of your relationship. This is the most difficult part for most people because there's a tendency to withhold the very thoughts that are the ones that need to be expressed.

You need to talk about your hopes as well as your fears. Sometimes it's even more difficult for a person to say, "I want to be rich and famous someday" (which is something James has said to me) than to say, "I'm afraid of growing old." But they are equally important. We only get to know each other by knowing our deepest feelings. So while it's important to learn to talk about everything that affects the relationship, don't focus *only* on the problems (even the major problem of affairs). The idea is to get to know each other better, more intimately. That means knowing what's going on inside, what makes you tick.

It's reasonable to ask your partner whatever you're curious about, but avoid absolutes in the form of demands or promises; they only serve to inhibit communication. Don't establish yourself as judge and jury of your partner. That's a sure way to keep them from sharing their thoughts and feelings. And don't be so deadly serious about the whole thing. Too much seriousness can kill a relationship. A little laughter (even at yourself) never hurts—and might help a great deal.

RESPONSIVENESS

Listening is just as important as talking in developing honest communication. You need to listen with your heart, not just your head. Try to hear the feelings behind the words, not just the words themselves. Listen patiently. Don't jump to conclusions and assume you know what the other person means without checking it out.

Listen quietly. If your partner shares a problem, this does not mean you should immediately try to solve it. Most people simply want their feelings to be heard; they don't want quick suggestions as to how to fix the problem. Usually, they don't want advice; they just want someone to understand how they feel. (A good source for learning more about this aspect of communication is a book titled *Human BE-ing* by Bill Pietsch.)

It's important to listen for information without immediately forming your own opinion of the "rightness" or "wrongness" of the information. Listen with acceptance. Don't tell the other person they shouldn't think or say whatever they've shared. This will only serve to cut off further sharing.

Try to listen without overreacting to disturbing thoughts or feelings. This, too, will have the effect of censoring future communication. Listen with appreciation for the sharing your partner has done. It isn't easy for many people to open up, and they need the encouragement that comes from having their efforts reinforced.

EXPECTATIONS

Expect resistance, both in yourself and in your partner; it's normal. But don't let it stop you from persisting at developing good communication. Expect to feel some strong emotions, but avoid blaming the other person for your feelings. Accept responsibility for your own feelings and emotions. Express your feelings by saying, "*I feel* so and so when you . . ." instead of saying, "*You* make me feel so and so when you . . ." This is a very subtle change, but it will give you a much better chance of being heard. A person who feels defensive at being blamed for your feelings won't be able to hear much of what you have to say.

Expect to feel some anxiety about answering your partner's questions, but don't let your anxiety stop you from trying to respond. Expect to want to withhold some of your feelings at times, but try to be honest about those feelings that are very strong and important to the relationship. You can't learn to really know each other if you hide your deepest feelings. Expect to feel fearful of changes these talks may bring about. But remember that change is inevitable, and the advantage of talking is that you get a chance to manage the change instead of having to adjust to whatever changes come your way. There's a tendency to focus only on the risk of talking, but sometimes there's far more risk in *not* talking.

Do expect some surprises, both good and bad. They're inevitable when you start talking more honestly.

Don't expect quick results. Be patient with yourself and your partner. Learning to develop a truly honest, intimate way of communicating will not happen overnight. But it *will* happen if both people make a persistent effort toward that goal.

Most couples have no appreciation of just how much communication is required to fully deal with their feelings about an affair. The long-term nature of this undertaking is well illustrated by the experience of one couple who worked for many years to finally reach this point. They had been married for fourteen years and had two children when she had an affair. She said she wasn't looking for it and can't quite explain how it happened. It lasted only a few months, and she turned back to her marriage with a renewed appreciation of her husband and the possibilities for their life together. She wanted to develop more honesty in their marriage and decided to tell her husband about her affair.

His initial reaction:

> *When my wife told me of her affair, I was devastated. But we are learning a great deal about what has been happening to us.*

One year later:

> *As honest as my wife is with me, as willing as she is to work through this, I know she is still holding back, first from herself and then from me.*

Six months later:

> *We are still having ups and downs but are learning a great deal about ourselves and each other. Sometimes it's fun, many times it's painful. Our relationship is clear of past affairs, and we're dealing with real problems of communication and finding out who we are.*

One year later:

> *We are doing very well in our relationship. She is in a therapy group and really likes it. We are also in marriage encounter groups.*

One year later:

> *We are still seeing a marriage counselor twice a month. Although we are working on our current relationship, the period of extramarital affairs still comes up. I still have some misunderstandings and resentments, and she just wants to forget it ever happened.*

Two years later:

> *We are out of counseling now. Our relationship is growing very nicely, and it's good to know we are able to handle upsets and problems and still grow closer.*

It might seem discouraging to think of this successful communication effort taking six years. But an awareness of the time and effort required should not be a deterrent. It should simply serve to provide hope at times when there's a tendency to become discouraged because things aren't happening as fast as you would like. It may help to think of how many people go through their entire lives without experiencing the satisfaction of real, intimate communication with their partner. Changing a lifetime pattern of communication is a major undertaking, but one with a tremendous payoff.

7

· · · · · · ·

Sexual Healing

Since an affair is by definition a sexual involvement with someone other than the primary partner, the discovery of an affair usually has a dramatic effect on a couple's sex life. Despite the fact that affairs happen for many reasons other than sexual ones, there is still a general feeling that there must have been a problem with the couple's sexual relationship for there to have been an affair in the first place. This is another of the many areas where an understanding of the nonpersonal, societal factors that contribute to affairs can help to heal the pain of this experience. But for most couples, the immediate issue is simply surviving the first blow of realizing a partner has had sex with someone else.

SEXUAL ALIENATION

· · · · · ·

For some couples, the discovery of an affair brings a temporary halt to their sex lives. Sometimes they continue to share the same bed, but avoid sexual contact. Others avoid sleeping in the same bed (or the same room). And still others report an intolerance of even being touched by the partner who had an affair. These situations may last for only one night or they may continue for several weeks or months. (And, of course, some couples never resume a normal sex life, eventually separating or getting a divorce.)

At a time like this, it's not unusual for someone who discovers their mate's affair to feel their mate is a stranger. Certainly, the idea of them as a person who has had sex with someone else is different from the earlier view. So part of the challenge is to get reacquainted with this "different" person, and this usually takes time. Patience can be an important key to getting through this period. It's especially important for the person who had an affair to be understanding and accepting of the time needed to adjust to what has happened.

For instance, if a woman resists sexual contact when she learns of her mate's affair, she may still be receptive to physical *comfort* (to being touched in a nonsexual way—having her hand held or being given a hug). This can serve to decrease the length of time she feels isolated and alienated. It can also make a difference if her partner shows compassion for her difficulty in dealing with this situation and does whatever he can to help her through it, including simple things like handling whatever joint responsibilities require attention during this period. Most women who are hurt and angry at their spouse may be reluctant to *ask* for this kind of practical help if their spouse doesn't offer any assistance, but it can serve to bridge the distance between them if this can happen.

Sometimes, a woman's lack of interest in sex has more to do with her feelings about herself than her feelings about her husband. Unfortunately, women have judged themselves so much in terms of their sexual desirability that the rejection they feel causes them to lose a sense of themselves as a sexual person and temporarily kills their own sexual desire. This attitude may also continue to affect a woman's feelings about sex once sexual activity is resumed. She may have "shut down" her feelings as a way of dealing with her pain, then find it difficult to become aroused and to have orgasms, even if this had never been a problem before. It may take time for her to regain her sexual confidence.

A similar problem can exist for a man who discovers his wife's affair. He may feel sexually threatened by the idea of comparisons with the other man or competitiveness about his sexual performance. One man was so preoccupied with wondering about the size of the other man's penis (but wouldn't ask his wife about it) and about his own stamina in comparison to the other man (although he didn't discuss that either) that sex became more stressful than pleasurable.

He began to doubt himself in ways he never considered before finding out about his wife's affair, which led him to go out and prove his sexual prowess by having sex with a number of other women. While his behavior wasn't motivated by a desire for revenge, she quite understandably interpreted it that way, and this compounded the original problem to a point where there was so much pain and anger on both sides that they decided it was too much to try to work through.

It's not unusual for a person to consider having an affair themselves after learning of their mate's affair. People have many different motives for this; it can be for revenge, of course, but it's more often the result of learning that this relationship, which they thought was monogamous, wasn't monogamous afer all. It's almost a "why not" attitude, since the pact has already been broken. Sometimes the desire to have an affair isn't even understood by the person who feels it.

I feel I am moving more and more toward the idea of having an affair myself, and it scares the hell out of me.

As mentioned earlier, the fact that their partner had an affair causes many people to feel a need to establish their sexual desirability, either with their mate or with someone else. If they feel sexually blocked with their mate, they may decide to try to revive their sexuality by having an affair.

It's not unusual for a man to react to his wife's affair by either leaving and never having sex with her again or reclaiming his sexual rights by insisting on constant sexual activity. If he chooses to leave, there's seldom anything she can do to change his mind. And if he decides to stay and overwhelm her with his sexuality, she will need to be understanding of his need to recover his sexual self-esteem. It's much more difficult when a man feels so threatened that he becomes impotent. But this, too, may only be a matter of time and patience in dealing with this stressful period while he comes to terms with the situation.

When a man discovers his wife's affair, his sexual feelings may become quite contradictory. On the one hand, his disbelief that his wife could have had an affair may dull his sexual feelings for her. He may have a sense of her as being "spoiled" by having engaged in sex with another man and is no longer sure he really *wants* her sexually. He may no longer see her as the wife he once loved and desired but as a repulsive person he doesn't know—and doesn't want to know.

On the other hand, it's possible for a man to have exactly the opposite reaction. One man described how his wife's affair made her *more* exciting to him sexually (as long as he focused on her strictly as a sex object), but less acceptable to him as a wife (because he no longer respected her). This kind of reaction is a carry-over of the double-standard thinking acquired by many men in the course of growing up—that the kind of woman who sleeps around is not the kind of woman you marry.

But it's not just men who may develop an increased sexual interest in their mate following the discovery of an affair. Several women reported their surprise and confusion at feeling very excited sexually and finding sex with their mate better than ever after finding out about their mate's affair. This can be a very strange experience, since it's happening at the same time they may feel anger, hurt, and uncertainty about the future.

However, this is not as strange as it may seem. Sex becomes highlighted in the course of focusing on an affair. Because of the attention to sexual behavior, there's a tendency to think in terms of sexual roles instead of the other roles that may normally be more dominant. This may lead to seeing a partner in a sexier light, causing them to seem more desirable. And since sex is the subject of such intense focus at this time, it can stimulate unexpected arousal.

PRACTICAL CONCERNS

While a man whose spouse has had an affair is struggling with his own personal pain, he may also be concerned as to whether the other man might have harmed his wife in any way. These feelings are based on his sense of responsibility to protect her because of his role as her husband. On the one hand, he doesn't want to think of the other man as kind or nice (or possessing any positive characteristic). But on the other hand, he doesn't want to think of his wife having had such a bad experience that it would harm their future sex life as a couple.

A woman whose husband has had an affair may have a slightly different set of concerns. She's seldom concerned about the man's physical well-being, but she may very well be concerned about her *own* because of his sexual involvement with other women. Following the discovery of an affair, many women insist that their husbands be tested for AIDS, especially if there's been a series of affairs. She doesn't want to have to deal with any physical trauma in addition to the emotional trauma she already feels. For some women this happens at the same time. One woman described how she found out about her husband's affair by discovering a lab report from a test he'd had done for venereal disease.

COPING WITH THE BARRIERS TO ENJOYMENT

For some couples, of course, there is a much less severe disruption of their lives and their relationship, including their sexual relationship. But even those couples who continue their sexual relationship often find that thoughts of the affair interfere with their ability to enjoy sex. The intensity of the emotional feelings about a partner's affair can block a person's sexual feelings. When they are dominated by feelings of anger and resentment, their bodies are in a state of tension that causes stress to the total system. Regardless of the basis of the stress, it tends to suppress sexual feelings.

The tension-related emotions associated with the pain of a partner's affair are usually restrictive, whereas those associated with sexual feelings are expansive. This creates a contradiction of feelings, usually blocking sexual expression. Since it takes time to overcome the negative feelings, one way to keep them from totally blocking any positive feelings is to try to transfer some of the emotional intensity from the negative feelings into sexual intensity. Several people have reported successfully making this transition.

It may take quite a while for some people to be able to engage in sex without feeling the presence of this "other person" as a barrier between them and their spouse. One woman whose husband had had an affair found a unique way to turn this around and use it to her advantage. She said that in the beginning whenever she and her husband had sex, the other woman was constantly "in bed with them" (in her mind), so she began to try imagining she was the other woman in order to enjoy it. Another wife found that by fantasizing about her husband having intercourse with the other woman, she was able to feel more sexual herself.

This may sound bizarre to the person who is not involved in the situation and is trying to apply reason or logic to these actions, but there's nothing rational about the feelings during this experience, including sexual feelings. People who feel sexually blocked by the idea of their partner having sex with someone else may be willing to try almost anything to help them recover their sexual feelings.

For most people, sexual reactions lie somewhere between the two extremes of no sex at all and an improvement in their sexual enjoyment. The particular reaction may depend to some extent upon the type of affair, but this has far less impact than most people assume. A one-night stand can feel just as devastating as a long-term involvement to the person trying to deal with it. Each individual has to cope with the facts of their particular situation, regardless of how it might compare to someone else's experience. And their feelings are likely to be as strong as those of another person in a seemingly more difficult situation.

EXAMINING OUR IDEAS ABOUT SEX
• • • • • •

Regardless of the particular situation, there's almost always a need for healing to take place before sex can become a satisfying experience again. And the first step toward this healing involves examining our attitudes and beliefs about sex and its place in our lives.

As long as things are going along reasonably well, we take for granted whatever sexual ideas we hold. Many times we aren't even aware of precisely what we think about sex because many of our ideas were developed as children when we accepted them without question. But the shock of dealing with extramarital affairs frequently gives rise to an analysis of just what it is we believe. Here's one woman's candid description of her early ideas about sex.

> *Because of being brought up to believe that sex is dirty and also because of some "bad" sexual experiences as a young girl, I found that I formed sort of an ideal love relationship in my head and determined that my relationship would make up for everything. Our lovemaking became sacred and very up on a pedestal. I couldn't imagine making love to anyone else or that anyone else even had a sexual relationship. Making love to him was the most beautiful thing in my life. Then when I found out about the affair, my "fairy-tale world" blew up, and I'd give all that I possess to have it back.*

Despite the fact that an affair can shatter old myths and dreams, it can also be an opportunity to learn for the first time some of the sexual realities for men and for women that neither sex has been aware of up until this time. It's not just a matter of men not understanding women and women not understanding men. Frequently, we don't have a clear understanding of our own attitudes about sex and how they came about. A closer look at some of the ways we develop our attitudes and beliefs about our sexuality can help us understand their influence on our thinking and our behavior.

GROWING UP MALE
· · · · · · ·

It's always risky to make general observations about men because, of course, there's a wide range of attitudes that exist among the male population. However, there are some general attitudes about sex that are worth noting when trying to assess this whole situation. Following are some of the common results of men's conditioning.

BEING PREOCCUPIED WITH SEX — EITHER DOING IT OR THINKING ABOUT IT

Long before there's any conscious awareness of sex, little boys begin playing with their penis. Since it's on the outside of their bodies, easily accessible, it's a source of enjoyment from the moment of birth. Sex educators have long recognized that this is a normal aspect of sexual development, and that erections occur even in the womb. Growing up, a focus on sex is an ongoing part of the male culture as they move through each successive step—from masturbation, curiously looking at women's bodies, and fantasizing, to finally "doing it."

SEPARATING SEX FROM LOVE

Boys grow up thinking of sex as a physical activity, not an emotional involvement. They understand that it's up to them to be the aggressor in whatever sexual activity is to take place. They get subtle (and not so subtle) reinforcement from older males. In some cultures older family members take responsibility for seeing that the adolescent males in their family have their first sexual experience by a certain age. While there's no formal system for a young man's introduction to sex in this society, there's ample approval of his early sexual exploration.

When one man on a recent television talk show commented that he had had his first sexual experience at age eleven, it prompted another man on the panel to say that he was the same age when it happened to him. They then reached over the people seated between them in order to shake hands on their shared experience. The public acceptance of this kind of disclosure demonstrates the degree to which we've come to expect the male's early pursuit of sexual activity (with no connection to love).

In their teen years, many boys who can't "make out" with a "nice" girl seek out a girl known as an "easy lay" in order to "get their first piece" (although they wouldn't want to be seen in public with her). When guys are hanging out together (especially if it's late at night following a date), the primary question they ask each other is, "Did you get any?" (This is not the case if the guy has a steady relationship where it's assumed to be more than just sex.) But it's no wonder that when a man grows up, it's difficult to overcome the separation that has always existed in his mind between sex and love. For many men, having affairs has nothing to do with love. In their minds, sex is a completely separate activity.

BEING PREOCCUPIED WITH THE SIZE OF THEIR PENIS AND HOW THEY COMPARE

Since public rest rooms for boys afford open viewing of others and male locker rooms have open showers and changing areas, boys are in the position of seeing others and seeing how they measure up. This preoccupation with size carries over into their relationships with women, causing concern if they think they're too small or exaggerated pride if they think they're exceptionally large. Most men are either unaware or unconvinced of the fact that penis size has nothing to do with most women's sexual satisfaction. Since the clitoris is the part of a woman's anatomy that is comparable to a man's penis, this is the primary source of her sexual pleasure, and orgasm is not a function of intercourse except as a by-product of the stimulation it provides to the clitoris.

SEEING WOMEN PRIMARILY AS SEX OBJECTS

As we've seen, the early sexual experience of most men leads them to grow up seeing women primarily as sex objects. But it's not just men who are conditioned to view women this way. This is a cultural process that is participated in by virtually everyone. The advertising media have led the way and reinforced this view in the way they use women to promote and sell almost every product and service available.

And, as unlikely as it may seem, women also learn to see themselves as sex objects to a certain degree. When little girls are small they are dressed up to be appealing; when they reach adolescence they dress to be noticed; and when they reach adulthood they dress to try to attract the attention and admiration of men. They recognize very early on that they have a special power over the opposite sex due to their desirability, and they play into this image of being a sex object almost unconsciously. So it's no wonder (with their own

conditioning and the cooperation of the media and women themselves) that most men see women primarily as sex objects.

WANTING TO HAVE SEX WITH A VARIETY OF WOMEN

There are many factors that lead to the desire of most men to have
sex with a lot of different women. While many people don't like
to consider that biology may play a part, studies done on rats have
verified what is called the Coolidge Effect—that male rats completely exhausted from copulation will become active again when
new females are introduced into their environment. Regardless of
whether human males have this kind of biological instinct, there
are plenty of societal and anthropological factors that have contributed to this preference for a variety of sexual partners.

Historically, there have been polygamous societies and centuries
of human development where it was critical that males "scatter
their seed" among a variety of childbearing women to carry on the
line and sustain the population of various groups. And there's the
influence of the double standard that still exists in the way boys
and girls are raised. As a society we've accepted a different standard
of sexual behavior for men and for women. For young women,
there's still a stigma attached to having sex with a variety of men
and a likelihood of getting a "bad reputation." But for young men,
having a large number of sexual encounters is seen as a normal part
of male adolescence.

Since young males tend to engage in sex with a variety of females,
they come to realize very early that there are many different types
of women, each with their own appeal, and they come to enjoy
and appreciate this variety. The desire for variety doesn't end with
marriage. Men who are completely candid about their ideal situation acknowledge that they would like to be married (with the
total life benefits of this partnership) and *also* to have sex with a
variety of other women. This has been widely reported, but most
people prefer to ignore this seemingly incongruous position.

Dr. Lewis Yablonsky reported in *The Extra-Sex Factor* that in his
study of over 800 men, "Married men, regardless of their 'extra-
sex,' seem to desire a base of their own with a family lifestyle,"

and that "Double-life men tend to love both a conventional family life and, additionally, an extra-sexual lifestyle."[1] In *Why Men Are the Way They Are*, Warren Farrell says, "The great majority of married men (three-fourths even in Kinsey's time) want extramarital relationships."[2]

People who say, "Why did he get married if he wanted to have affairs" fail to understand this basic desire for both marriage *and* sexual variety. This doesn't mean men always act on this wish, but it does help if we recognize that this preference exists.

USING SEX AS EVIDENCE OF POWER AND CONQUEST

The pure pleasure of the sex act is not the only satisfaction most men find in sexual activity; sex also increases their feelings of power and of being in control of their lives. Many men get so hooked on the excitement of the pursuit and conquest that they quickly lose interest after they succeed. Women who wonder why a man doesn't call or pursue them after a first encounter fail to recognize the degree to which the chase is the thing. Closely associated with the satisfaction of successfully catching a woman is the enjoyment of telling other men about it. If men were not able to brag about their conquests to other men, it would somewhat diminish the pleasure of their success.

FEELING THEIR PARTNER ''OWES'' THEM SEX

Once courtship results in a commitment, men tend to feel this establishes their "right" to have sex. This is far more likely to be the case in marriage than in other kinds of relationships. Peter Kreitler, a marriage counselor and author of *Affair Prevention*, wrote about this issue in describing his work with married men: "Many married men judge their sex life by how many notches they cut on the bedpost each week. They will often admit, in the privacy of my office, 'I need to get laid more.' Men have been much more direct about determining their need for an affair by how much sex they have with their wife."[3]

It's quite common for a man to feel justified in having an affair if his wife doesn't give him the sex he feels she "owes" him. Unfortunately, lack of sex at home has come to be a somewhat *acceptable* explanation (both in his own eyes and in the eyes of society as a whole), but the real attraction to outside sex has less to do with the quality and quantity of sex at home than with the novelty and excitement of sex with someone new.

The tendency to take sex for granted and see it as something that is "owed" does not help to stimulate a rewarding sex life for either men or women. Our unrealistic images of the amount of sex we should have and the degree of excitement it should bring tend to interfere with sexual enjoyment within a committed relationship.

GROWING UP FEMALE
· · · · · · ·

Many of the factors that affect women's attitudes toward sex in normal times are simply exaggerated when faced with their partner's affair. Their feelings about sex in this situation are significantly affected by their conditioning, not just about sex, but about how to relate to men in general. While not representative of *all* women, following are some of the common issues that women bring to their feelings about sex.

SEEING SEX AS CONFIRMATION OF THEIR WORTH

Women have been conditioned to see sex as something through which they get confirmation and reassurance of their worth. While the man's focus is on the woman and how much he wants her, the woman's focus is not likely to be on wanting him. She's also focusing on how much he wants her. Women are more interested in being wanted than in wanting. Her conditioned need for admiration and approval simply overshadows her sex drive unless she learns to overcome her dependence on others to determine her sense of self-worth.

SEEING MEN AS THE INSTIGATORS OF SEX

While women have been conditioned to try to be appealing and sexually desirable, they also learned as little girls that they should control their own sexual urges. They learned that boys would make sexual advances and they should resist (or at least restrict the degree of involvement). Then when they get married, women are expected to be sexually liberated, able to initiate sex and to thoroughly respond to their mate's overtures. But their conditioning often interferes with successfully making this change in their thinking and behavior.

Women usually continue to see men as the instigators of sex and themselves as prepared to respond to the man's overtures. This idea of being ready to respond "in case" he wants sex is a great distraction to being in touch with whether or not a woman wants it herself. I can remember times when I might have eaten a light meal or shaved my legs when I thought my husband was going to initiate sex, but didn't necessarily suggest it myself if he didn't.

This tendency to wait for men to initiate sex is part of a traditional pattern of thinking of men as the initiators at each stage of the relationship, from asking for a date, to "making the first move," to proposing marriage. These old attitudes of seeing the man as the initiator are changing as more women become comfortable with expressing their own preferences and desires.

WANTING EVERYTHING JUST RIGHT FOR SEX

Women tend to want everything to be "just right" for sex. This means plenty of time, privacy, and a romantic mood. It also means avoiding the many distractions that can interfere with her ability to enjoy sex—such as kids, tight schedules, other responsibilities, physical tiredness, etc. Holding too rigidly to these standards interferes with spontaneity and causes the sexual relationship to suffer.

For some women, the list of things that can interfere is endless. One woman told of her growing problem with being able to relax and enjoy sex only when she was assured of total privacy. It began with her being uncomfortable having sex when her parents were visiting (even though she was married and her parents were in another part of the house). The next step was to be uncomfortable having sex when the children were in the house (unless she was sure they were asleep). Then, as the children got older and stayed up as late as she did, she was uncomfortable having sex unless the kids were away from home. At this point, she sought help and eventually was able to overcome her extreme requirements for having everything "just right" for sex.

BEING JUDGMENTAL OF THEIR PHYSICAL APPEARANCE

Women are so judgmental of their own bodies that their focus on whether they're too fat or whether their breasts are too small (or whatever part of their body they don't like) interferes with their ability to focus on what they're feeling. This preoccupation with their looks causes many women to restrict their nudity (and their availability for sex) to nighttime, preferably with the lights out. Whenever there's light, whether daylight or artificial light at night, there's a different kind of attention paid to their body and how it looks in various positions. The media presentation of what a sexy woman is supposed to look like has resulted in many women *feeling* sexy only if they think they *look* sexy.

INCLUDING SEX ON THEIR LIST OF RESPONSIBILITIES

Some women tend to see sex as one item on a long list of activities for which they're responsible. Many have a checklist in their heads of all the things they're supposed to take care of and keep up to date, and one of these items is sex. Their thinking goes something like this:

> I finished that project at work (Check);
> I attended the kids' program at school (Check);
> I got all the bills paid on time (Check);
> I bought groceries and prepared a nice dinner (Check);
> I had sex with my husband (Check)!

Any of these responsibilities that is not fulfilled in a timely way creates a feeling of failure or inadequacy.

PUTTING OTHERS' NEEDS FIRST

Women have been trained to believe that others' needs should be served before their own. But when it comes to sex, even if they do a good job of performing, a man knows on some level that something's missing when the only concern is his satisfaction. He may not know specifically when orgasms are faked—apparently many men can be fooled about this, partly because they want to believe they're real—but he'll know things aren't quite what he wishes they were. Of course, a good sexual relationship depends on *both* partners' satisfaction.

BEING UNWILLING TO BE VULNERABLE

Women aren't willing to be vulnerable and let themselves go when they feel uncertain or anxious or resentful toward their partner. Many women who have difficulty with orgasms when involved with their partner (but who easily have orgasms through self-stimulation when they're alone) think it's because they know how to stimulate themselves in ways men don't. A more likely reason for this difference is that orgasms occur naturally when she feels "safe" enough to let her body freely do what it feels like doing, but for many women the degree of trust and openness is not sufficient to allow them to be completely vulnerable with their partner. This is especially true when a woman is trying to recover from her partner's affair.

SOME EFFECTS OF THE DIFFERENCES
· · · · · · ·

The bottom line of the differences in conditioning between males and females is that women have been conditioned to use sex to get approval and admiration from men, while men have been conditioned to show affection in order to get sex from women. This conditioning, of course, is general and does not apply to every man and woman. But it does provide insight into the possible effects of extramarital affairs on the two sexes. Men are more likely to feel rejected *sexually*, while women are more likely to feel rejected in a more general way *as a person*.

Sexual healing following an affair involves not only understanding the effects of our attitudes about sex, but being willing to change those that interfere with our ability to enjoy a satisfying sex life. For instance, most men grow up seeing sex and pleasure as very closely connected. But women often see sex primarily as a symbol of love and commitment, with pleasure being somewhat less important. If both are willing to reevaluate their attitudes, it can lead to finding a common ground of recognition of both the loving and pleasurable aspects of sex.

One woman (who realized that she saw sex as a very "serious" aspect of her marriage) made a deliberate effort to change this way of thinking after discovering her husband's affair.

> *I've tried hard to "lighten up" my serious approach to sex only as an expression of love—and I feel I've succeeded somewhat. I find that I enjoy sex much more now since I am trying to look at it as "sex for pleasure."*

Coming to an appreciation of sex for pleasure can help in understanding some of the appeal of an affair (since this is the way sex is viewed in most affairs). Since extramarital sex is disassociated from the responsibilities of commitment and involvement in other aspects of life, it becomes a focal point of attention in a more prominent way than in most marriages. But a recognition of the sheer fun that can *also* be a part of marital sex can help to heal the wounds following an affair.

This involves recognizing the nonsexual factors that can interfere with sexual pleasure. Since women still bear the major burden of the daily household hassles (and since sex usually takes place in the home environment where she's trying to deal with these hassles), she is likely to have a difficult time setting aside these distractions and focusing on sex. And her feelings of resentment that her husband hasn't shared more of these routine responsibilities (that have nothing to do with sex) can have a tremendous effect on her sexual feelings and sexual pleasure. Also, her tendency to associate sex with love means that anything causing her to feel unloved or uncared-for may affect her sexual feelings.

It's easy to see how the contrast between the wife's attitudes (seeing sex as a symbol of love, wanting everything "just right" for sex, and including sex on her list of responsibilities) and the husband's attitudes (being preoccupied with sex, seeing sex as pleasure, and feeling his wife "owes" him sex) can create problems. A reevaluation of these sexual attitudes can significantly benefit a couple's efforts to establish a good sex life following an affair.

FINDING WAYS TO HEAL
· · · · · · ·

While an affair itself almost always causes severe damage to a couple's sex life, the challenge is to use this experience as a catalyst to work toward developing a more satisfying sexual relationship. James and I finally managed to reach that point after going through many years while his affairs drove us further and further apart sexually. During the seven years when he was actually involved in affairs (and when I suspected without knowing for sure), I lost touch with my own sexual feelings; I was too busy pretending, testing, and competing with whatever other women he might be having sex with.

Then when he told me about his affairs, it created a real breakthrough in our sex life. Surprisingly, we made love a couple of hours after he told me about his many affairs. His honesty that night provided such a relief from the anxiety I'd suffered during all those years of wondering that I felt a closeness that hadn't been possible while dominated by feelings of doubt and suspicion. However, this turned out to be a temporary high before settling in to the long process of dealing with the full impact of his affairs.

In the months following the night I learned about his affairs, I felt a lingering sense of sadness that the specialness of our sex was now gone. Sometimes I would feel so subdued that I would be unable to let go and get in touch with my sexual feelings. But even during those times when I wasn't able to bring a great deal of enthusiasm to the sex act, I continued to engage in sex because I wanted to overcome these feelings of distance and continue to build the relationship. At other times, I would become fully aroused and completely enjoy our lovemaking, only to be lying in his arms afterward and have a sinking feeling just sweep over me as I thought about some other woman lying in his arms like that.

Many women have shared similar frustrations at their fluctuating sexual feelings after their husband's affair. The intensity of these feelings and the length of time they persist depend to a great extent on what else is happening in the relationship, specifically the degree of trust and honesty that has been developed. My own period of sexual adjustment following James's affairs was much shorter because of the trust I had that he was not continuing to have affairs after that night when he told me about them.

HONESTY

Honesty can lead to a level of trust that can have the wonderful by-product of making a couple's sex life far richer and more exciting than it ever was before. This is a very important feature of honesty (one that many people overlook)—that it creates excitement in a relationship, especially in the area of sex. A couple can feel safe enough to be completely vulnerable with all their desires, fears, and insecurities.

For instance, during the earlier years of our marriage, I (like many women) occasionally faked orgasms. I never do that anymore. If I don't have an orgasm, I feel no pressure (either for my sake or his) to pretend otherwise. I've also learned that I can almost always have an orgasm if I do whatever *I* need to do to have one instead of waiting and hoping he does the "right" thing.

So the initial impact of affairs on a couple's sex life doesn't necessarily indicate the final results. It all depends on what happens during this healing process and how open they can be about what they want and need. Sometimes the sexual relationship can become even better than it was before. Unfortunately, some people use this fact as a rationalization to justify an affair—that it provides some benefit to the marriage. It's clear that James's affairs didn't *help* our sex life. Our sex life improved because of the work we did to overcome the affairs and because of the honesty we developed in working through the pain and misunderstandings.

COMMUNICATION

While there are many factors that play a part in regaining some sense of normalcy in sexual relationships following an affair, this opening up the lines of communication about sex is one of the most important. Sometimes this involves sharing old hurts and disappointments that have been kept secret. For instance, one man told of finally telling his wife about his feelings of sexual deprivation over the years. He had felt inadequate and rejected, but she never suspected these feelings because he had usually responded to her avoidance of sex by criticizing and attacking her, while hiding his deeper feelings of hurt. Once he expressed his true feelings, she felt much more loving and caring—and much more inclined to engage in sex. While it was difficult for him to share this with her (and difficult for her to hear the pain and rejection he expressed), it provided the basis for a new understanding of each other's feelings about sex, thereby leading to a new level of closeness.

The sharing of hidden feelings, however, needs to be done with a great deal of care if it's to work for the benefit of the relationship. One woman learned this the hard way when she failed to recognize the importance of the manner and timing of this kind of honesty. In the midst of a frustrating sexual encounter, she blurted out the fact that she didn't know why she bothered to have sex since she never had orgasms and had faked them for years. Her husband was enraged (feeling she was saying he was a lousy lover) and humiliated that he had been "conned" for such a long time. They finally worked through this initial damage, but it could have been avoided by a more thoughtful way of sharing the information.

The resolution of sexual problems following an affair can take many forms. Sadly, some couples come to an accommodation of the fact that sex will no longer be a part of the relationship. Many people find this inconceivable. They can't imagine staying in a relationship without sex. They think it would be better not to be together at all. But the number of couples living in sexless marriages is greater than most people realize, and it's not for us to judge whether or not they would be better off apart. Sometimes other factors are more important to a given couple than sex.

For instance, the wife of a man who had had an affair explained that her husband was the one who chose to eliminate sex from their lives. He was unwilling to talk about it or to go to counseling. So it was up to her to leave if she couldn't accept the situation. They had been married for thirty-five years. She said they were good friends, lived together well, and were great company for each other. So she decided there was nothing to be gained by leaving and much to be lost. She said she had adjusted to the situation and felt they were going to make it.

MAKING SEX BETTER
· · · · · · ·

For those who do see sex as important and genuinely want to do whatever they can to improve their sex life, one of the simplest, most practical things to do is to turn off the television and go to bed—together. Better still, establish certain periods when the television isn't even turned on. It's amazing how many people say they don't have time for sex, when they spend countless hours watching television.

Despite the romantic illusion that sex should "just happen," it deserves to be included in the schedule just like any other important part of life. People having affairs certainly plan for sex; it's an essential part of the process. So, too, should people in monogamous relationships. This attention to planning doesn't preclude having spontaneous sex. One way to increase the likelihood of more spontaneous sex is to pay attention to other things that bring feelings of closeness, like listening to each other, helping each other with problems, speaking in a gentle tone instead of with impatience or irritability, and generally creating a climate of caring.

THE HEALING POWER OF TOUCH

An important part of the process of developing a feeling of closeness and caring is through comforting and touching each other in non-sexual ways. One of the most positive changes in my own relationship since struggling with the issue of affairs has been developing a habit of more constant physical contact with my husband, primarily as a way of staying "connected." We start by spending about fifteen minutes when we first wake up, just cuddling and being close. This may or may not lead to sex. It's not done for sexual reasons; it's simply starting the day with the kind of positive feelings that come from this kind of closeness. And we continue this attention to physical contact at other times during the day.

The importance of touch has long been established as essential to the development of infants. But all of us can benefit from the healing power of touch. Here's a portion of a poem James wrote about the experience of touch and its place in our lives. While this writing obviously means a lot to me personally, I want to share it because of its potential for raising awareness of the importance of this basic human need.

Skin on Skin
by James Vaughan

When all the dust has settled, it's touch that counts.
    A smile is nice.
    So is good conversation
        and an approving look.
But when the chips are down, it's touch we crave,
    and touch that tells us most clearly
        where we stand with another person.
Skin on skin . . .
    That's where we begin,
    and where we end.
Strange—that the finest gift a human being can give another
    gets blocked so often by fear.
Strange—and sad—that so many people go through day after day
    feeling alone and alienated,
        when the solution to their dilemma is so simple
        and so close at hand.
We can change our lives and the lives of those around us
    by reaching out and touching.

Increasing the amount of touch can make a tremendous difference, not only in a sense of well-being, but also in feeling inclined to engage in sex. Foreplay doesn't begin in bed just prior to intercourse; it begins in the morning and continues throughout the day. The kind of foreplay I'm referring to involves not only touching, but talking, being responsive to each other, and just generally being connected in a way that leads to feeling close. When these things are missing, there's a very different effect, leading to feelings of resentment and distance that interfere with being interested in sex.

As discussed earlier, men have been conditioned to be capable of separating sex from other aspects of life somewhat more than women. Also, they have learned through business or team sports to be able to compartmentalize their lives and participate in events with others, even when there are tensions or disagreements. So they may be able to set aside feelings of conflict with their mates enough to still feel interested in sex. But women tend to integrate the various aspects of their lives, so that nonsexual problems create a definite dampening of their sexual feelings. For both sexes, however, outside events affect both the frequency and pleasure of sex.

Because of the feelings of closeness from more physical contact outside the bedroom, there's likely to be a dramatic increase in enthusiasm when it comes to sexual activity. This is especially true for women, since their conditioning has given them so many preoccupations that interfere with sexual enjoyment. And since most men enjoy sex more when the woman is enjoying it too, this can make the sexual experience more satisfying for both partners.

RECLAIMING WHATEVER WAS LOST

A common problem for many couples is the feeling that certain acts or experiences may be so closely related to the affairs that they seem to be ruined for the primary sexual relationship. But this doesn't have to be the case. For instance, since oral sex was the central feature of one of the affairs my husband had (before it became a regular part of our sex life), it would have been easy to feel that this was now ruined for us, that this would forever be a reminder of that affair. Instead of letting that happen, we deliberately focused on it as part of our lovemaking, thereby "owning" it for ourselves. So instead of shying away from it or avoiding it because of the other association, we diluted the importance of the other experience and made it eventually fade away by replacing it with our own.

Another common legacy of an affair is that the atmosphere is usually more romantic than the home environment. One woman was distressed at the image of her husband having had most of his sexual encounters with the other woman in nice hotels on trips, while their sexual activity usually took place at home in very "unromantic" surroundings. They didn't have the money to take more than an occasional vacation, but this longing for more interesting locations led them to find places other than their home to have sex.

For instance, one of the most exciting places they found was in the husband's office on weekends when no one else was there. It wasn't specifically planned, but they would go out for lunch and he would just happen to need to go by the office for something— and they would seize the opportunity. The idea that they occasionally heard voices from some of the other offices in the large office building only added to their delight at the idea that someone might actually hear their "noises" and suspect what was going on.

While this example may seem to reinforce the idea of looking for ways to "spice up" a couple's sex life (like going to a motel with no luggage and wearing sexy underwear), this is not the case. There's been far too much emphasis on these artificial inducements to exciting sex—and far too little attention to the more natural contributors to good sex (like honesty, communication, and a great deal more touch). As mentioned earlier, the primary way to create and sustain excitement in a sexual relationship is through honesty. It provides a sense of newness and surprise that can't be matched by any of the standard gimmicks for improving a couple's sex life.

NOT ALL WOUNDS CAN BE HEALED

Of course, some sexual problems that result from affairs are much more serious and not as amenable to being overcome, much less turning into something positive. For instance, several people reported that an affair had resulted in pregnancy. In one case, a woman said she had known for some time that her husband was having affairs but had chosen to ignore it and go on with her life. But when one of the other women became pregnant and confronted him with the fact that she did not want to have an abortion, he panicked and turned to his wife for advice and comfort. This was the last straw, and she divorced him. She said she actually felt sorry for him, but she couldn't stand around and watch him mess up his life (and hers) any longer.

In one very unusual case, when a pregnancy resulted from an affair, the wife of the man having the affair was presented with the option of adopting the child into their own home or having her husband leave her and marry the woman who was going to have his child. It seems the other woman was young and poor and had neither the desire nor the ability to raise the child. But since the couple had no children, her husband wanted this child and preferred that he and his wife raise it together. His wife was a "foreign bride" who had no other relatives or resources in this country (and still loved her husband and had wished for a child), so she decided to stay with him and take the child into their home as their own.

This is a unique situation, one that most of us cannot quite comprehend, but it's important to acknowledge that affairs create circumstances that have no simple solutions. The challenge for each person is to determine the best way for them to recover from this experience. Regardless of the particular path a person chooses, it's likely to be a difficult process. In the course of trying to heal from the experience of a partner's affair, most people seek some kind of outside help, which is the next issue we'll consider.

8

. . . .

Where and How to Get Help

In the first shock of discovering a mate's affair, many people have a desperate need to turn to someone for immediate comfort and support. The irony of this situation is that they can't turn to the person they would normally lean on in a crisis situation (since it's this person's affair that has caused the crisis). So most people turn first to friends or other family members.

SUPPORT FROM FRIENDS AND FAMILY
. . . .

When a person turns to a friend for help, it's important that they get the kind of help they need. The clearer a person can be about what they need from a friend at this time, the more likely they are to get it. For instance, if all they need is to avoid being alone and to have someone listen, it's important that they say so. If they want to be distracted by other activities, that, too, needs to be expressed. If they want their friend's opinion of what they should do, they need to ask for it. And if they *don't* want advice, they need to be clear in letting their friend know that as well. Without this kind of guidance, a friend might respond in a way that is precisely opposite from what is needed.

Unfortunately, even with the best of intentions, most people can't seem to resist the temptation to give advice. Typically, they say, "I think you should . . ." or "If it were me, I'd . . ." But nobody knows what they would do unless and until it *is* them, so they shouldn't offer their opinions unless specifically asked. A person usually feels terribly weakened when they find out their mate has had an affair, and they need to develop strength and confidence in their ability to cope with this situation, which doesn't happen by having someone else tell them what they should do.

I find there are drawbacks in confiding in even intimate friends in that they try to impose their values on the situation and can leave you feeling even worse.

Being given unsolicited advice by a friend places an unnecessary burden on a person already overburdened; they may feel that if they reject the advice, it will put a strain on the friendship. A person may feel inclined to stop associating with friends who seem unable or unwilling to keep their opinions to themselves.

While turning to a relative for help is not likely to carry the same risk to the relationship, there's a different kind of risk involved. A relative's sense of this situation as a "family" problem may cause them to feel so *personally* involved that they get caught up in their own feelings about the affair. They may have their own very strong opinions about what the person should do and may feel even more justified in giving advice.

For the friend or family member who wants to be helpful to a person struggling with their mate's affair (but doesn't know how), there are some simple things to keep in mind. First, they need to ask what the person needs. If they can't identify any big ways to be helpful, there are many small ways to make a difference. Frequently, a person needs help in coping with their daily responsibilities—shopping, babysitting, etc.—and any relief from these routine matters will be greatly appreciated.

Also, they need to be distracted by other things in life that are meaningful to them (that they may have ignored since discovering their mate's affair). This does not mean trying to get them to forget about the affair; nothing will make it go away. But it can be lifesaving to focus on other things that can provide some relief from the constant focus on this problem.

One of the most important benefits of talking to friends and family is simply that it helps most people break through the sense of isolation they feel at this time. When friends and family can simply "be there" for those who need their support, this can play an important part in the healing process.

I have a very supportive friend who never criticizes me and never tries to tell me what to do or not to do.

I have discussed it with several friends (who have been terrific) and my mother (and she's been terrific).

PROFESSIONAL HELP
• • • • • • •

While friends and family can be helpful in surviving the immediate impact of learning of a mate's affair, most people feel the need for professional help in sorting through what has happened and determining what to do about the situation. Most of the people in BAN had sought some kind of counseling. They reported a wide range of results, which is understandable because there's such a wide range of sources for professional help. There are counselors, therapists, psychologists, and, of course, the clergy. They have varying degrees of training and ability to deal with this issue.

There are a number of understandable reasons for the variability in professional help besides the differences in training. There's also the potential impact of personal experience. Since this issue touches every facet of society, professionals are not exempt from having to deal with affairs in their own lives (either having had an affair themselves or having a partner who had an affair). Those professionals who have dealt with affairs personally can't completely escape being affected by their experience, which, in turn, may have an impact on their professional approach to dealing with this issue.

Regardless of their experience, one approach that is shared by most professionals is that of exploring with a couple what weaknesses or problems within each person and within each particular relationship caused one of the partners to have an affair. Since this approach forms the basis for most professional help, it reinforces the idea that affairs are due strictly to personal inadequacies. This practice of identifying who or what is to "blame" for the affair often creates additional problems.

For instance, one woman told of going to a counselor who said (after two sessions) that her husband was "sufficiently" guilt-ridden and sorry about what he'd done, and that if the marriage fell apart now, she could take the total blame for it as well as for ruining the rest of their kids' lives. She was so frustrated by this turn of events that she pleaded with her husband to go to a different counselor. Ironically, the second counselor continued the theme of placing "blame," this time determining that her husband was totally to blame and recommending that she get a divorce immediately. When she again became extremely distressed, the counselor suggested Valium for her nerves. By this time, she was too afraid to even try a third counselor. Unfortunately, this kind of difficult experience with counselors happens more often than it should, according to the many reports I received from BAN members.

Of course, some people have a very positive experience with counseling. For many couples, counseling was not only helpful, but *essential* to their being able to deal with this problem. In most of these instances, the people felt their emotional stability was in much better shape after the counseling. Especially satisfying was the report of one couple who said it appeared their love and marriage would weather the storm and be much stronger because of their commitment to honesty. Some couples wondered how anyone could possibly get through this experience without professional help.

Finding the right counselor can be quite a challenge, and there's no simple solution as to how to go about it. Often, there's no way to determine in advance whether or not the counseling experience will provide the kind of positive help that's possible. Here are some guidelines that might be helpful in choosing a counselor and in assessing the progress of the counseling experience.

HOW TO BENEFIT FROM PROFESSIONAL HELP
• • • • • • •

Go to a counselor who has been personally recommended by someone who has used them and whose opinion is trusted. (This, of course, means being willing to let others know of the need to find a counselor.) This recommendation should not be the overriding determination, of course, but this "personal" impression can provide additional input to consider along with an assessment of the professional qualifications.

Consider the sex of the counselor. For couples, there's always the possibility of receiving counseling from a male/female team of professionals, which resolves any issue as to the sex of the counselor. If a couple goes to a single counselor, it will be beneficial if they can agree on the sex of the counselor. If not, they will need to "test" their experience with either a male or female counselor and evaluate their feelings about the experience, being open to considering the other alternative.

If a person is going to counseling alone, the decision, of course, is completely up to them. Some people feel more comfortable with a same-sex counselor, while others prefer someone of the opposite sex. And still others may have no clear preference. But if the sex of the counselor is likely to affect a person's receptivity to help, they need to acknowledge this in advance and avoid any unnecessary drawbacks to the process.

Be willing to "interview" counselors or "shop around." Most people are uncomfortable with the idea of questioning a professional because of their tendency to be intimidated by the professional's training and expertise. All too often, people waste time, money, and emotional energy rather than question the judgment of a professional. Second opinions are gaining wide acceptance in the medical field, but it's still difficult for people to act on this principle, especially when dealing with an emotional issue like affairs.

Nevertheless, the wide range of differences in individual needs and in professional abilities and attitudes certainly makes it wise to approach counseling in a businesslike way. It's reasonable to view the first session as a time for all parties concerned to evaluate the potential for working together before committing to an ongoing relationship. Compatibility is very important to successful counseling, as is the degree of comfort with the professional and the degree of confidence in their ability to be helpful.

Find a counselor who believes in honesty and encourages honest communication. The first step, of course, is for the couple to determine whether they want to strive for honest communication about all aspects of this issue and to develop an honest relationship. If this is the case, then it's important to find a counselor who will reinforce this effort. Since many counselors believe there's a danger in too much honesty, this is an issue that will need to be discussed to determine whether an agreement can be reached as to the goals of counseling in this regard.

Clarify goals to find the best fit. Honesty is only one of the issues to be resolved in terms of the goals of counseling. A couple also needs to be as clear as possible as to whether their primary goal is to stay together or to achieve the best *personal* recovery, regardless of whether or not that involves staying together. They should also consider whether their goal is to achieve a good understanding of what happened or to put it behind them as quickly as possible without striving for much understanding of the situation.

They need to communicate their goals to the counselor to determine if the counselor is comfortable in helping them work toward achieving those goals. It's important to know if a therapist uses some particular method that is incompatible with this kind of partnership approach to treatment.

Ask about the counselor's view of affairs as more than just a personal issue. Since the counselor's thinking on this point may not become clear until some time into the counseling process, it may be necessary to ask about their approach. In some instances, however, there will be clues as to their thinking based on whether their guidance in exploring the situation focuses exclusively on problems within the marriage as causing the affair.

As discussed earlier, most professionals tend to focus only on the personal factors involved in affairs without including an evaluation of the experience in the context of society as a whole. A purely personal focus reinforces the idea of personal blame, whereas a societal perspective can help overcome some of the negative focus on blaming, thereby diminishing the emotional impact and increasing the ability to deal with the issues to be resolved. **Be aware of feelings of strength or weakness that result from working with the counselor.** If a counselor is too quick with absolutes or advice, this can interfere with a person's ability to think through their situation and deal with their problems. In fact, this approach can create additional problems on top of the ones they're already trying to deal with. Also, if the counselor is critical of a person's need to talk about their feelings or to ask questions of their spouse, this can interfere with their struggle to overcome the damage to their self-esteem.

The work with the counselor should have the effect of *empowering* a person, making them feel more confident and better able to deal with the situation, not overly dependent on the professional. It's important to listen to whatever advice professionals have to offer, but not to assume they know precisely what's best. They can give guidance, but not answers.

Do not be afraid to stop seeing a counselor whenever things are not going according to the general considerations listed above. If there is basic disagreement about some of these issues, it's important to discuss the areas of disagreement with the counselor to determine whether they can be resolved, or to acknowledge that there isn't a good fit in this particular counseling effort. With the enormous differences in individuals and in counselors, it often requires a trial and error period to find the best possible fit.

There is no need to feel a sense of failure (either as the client or as the professional) when this happens. Both parties need to be willing to stop at any point, after the first session or the tenth. It's especially important to avoid a long-term association that creates dependence without demonstrating progress in becoming more capable of functioning without professional help.

SUPPORT GROUPS

· · · · · · ·

Even if a person receives help through counseling, support groups can play an important part in the healing process. (In fact, some counseling takes place in a group setting.) But if a person is not in counseling, it's even more essential to get some kind of outside support.

THE BENEFITS OF SUPPORT GROUPS

One of the most powerful benefits of support groups is their ability to break through the sense of isolation that many people feel when dealing with affairs. Most people tend to withdraw from life and from interactions with others, and even the prospect of talking to others who share the same experience can be frightening. One woman described sitting in her car in the parking lot for fifteen minutes before getting up her nerve to go in to her first support group meeting.

When she finally did go inside, she was surprised to find that thoughts and emotions she thought were uniquely hers were shared by others. For a long time she sat quietly listening to others in the group, then finally spoke up to say that she had been secretly convinced that no one had ever felt the pain she had felt, but now she knew she wasn't alone.

Others commented on how good it felt to talk to someone who had "been there." They found it comforting to have others say, "I know what you are going through. I've been there myself." This often creates a bond of common understanding that gives a person strength to face their own problems. Here's the way one person reflected on the healing benefit of this kind of group sharing.

> *As I look back on our meeting, I realize that not one of us said, "Do you know what I mean?" We all knew. What a relief, knowing that someone understands—really understands.*

Another benefit of the meetings is that a person can gain a perspective of their situation that isn't possible when dealing with it alone. They see other people at different stages of recovery; they see some who are at a similar stage to their own, some who are better off, and some who are having a much more difficult time at that point. Due to this variability, support groups provide an opportunity for people to give as well as receive. When people are struggling with a mate's affair, they tend to feel weak and powerless. Frequently, they can regain some strength and confidence by helping others who are going through the same thing. Sometimes those who have survived this experience and want to reach out in supporting others are frustrated because there's no clear way to go about it. Even tentative efforts to open up the subject for discussion may be met with uncomfortable silence, if not outright resistance.

> *Why is everyone so afraid to discuss affairs? They want to close it up—not hear me or share themselves. Ignore it and it will go away and not touch us. Have a happy life and all will live happily ever after. It is so frustrating—but I haven't give up.*

It's always hard when people are breaking new ground and trying to go against the prevailing norms. It's not easy to speak out about personal experiences when society is saying it's not appropriate to do that. If those who want to be of help are to have any realistic chance of making a difference, it's up to all of us to help create a climate that makes it acceptable to discuss these issues more openly. It's a delicate subject, but it's time we made an effort to support those who are willing to speak out.

It took me several years to begin discussing my own experience. I didn't just wake up one day and decide to pour out my whole story. It was a very gradual process of telling a few people and getting such positive reinforcement for the value of the sharing that I increasingly expanded my openness in talking about it. This open discussion has been an extremely satisfying experience. My efforts to help others led to increasing my understanding and perspective of what had happened in my own life. The common bond of recognizing similarities in individual feelings and reactions is a great help in overcoming the sense of being so alone.

> *I feel a person shouldn't go through this alone—and it helps to have someone say, I know, I've been there, and I care. How do we reach those people who are too frightened to come out?*

My life has restabilized now, and I feel a sincere obligation to those people who are "eating my dust" to spare them some of the frustration and misery I went through.

HOW TO FORM A SUPPORT GROUP

Ideally, a person could simply look in the phone book and find a support group for people dealing with affairs. There are organized groups for many other problems facing society today (alcoholism, child abuse, rape, drug addiction, spouse abuse, etc.), but there is no national organization devoted specifically to dealing with this issue. This is yet another illustration of the degree of secrecy surrounding affairs. It's one of the most prevalent problems in society today, but it's still not formally recognized as a legitimate societal issue.

As to specific ways to go about forming a support group, there is no set method for how to get started. Sometimes all it takes is one person who is willing to openly acknowledge they have dealt with this issue personally. It's possible to reach others by sharing your own experience and having people respond who might not otherwise have admitted they were dealing with this issue. Since I had openly discussed my experience and heard from others as a result, I was able to put people in touch with each other who lived in areas close enough to meet. Then they took responsibility for arranging a meeting in a public place to get acquainted and determine where to go from there.

In other instances, BAN members used a variety of methods to form local groups when there were no other members in their area. In one case, they called their local newspaper and offered an anonymous "interview" about affairs in which they talked about their own experience and about the need for people to come together to talk about their feelings. When the paper ran the article, they included an address for people to write if they'd had this experience and were interested in being part of a support group. This mail was collected by the one who gave the interview, who then called the others and set up a meeting.

Another effort involved asking a clergyman to serve as a go-between. He announced the establishment of a support group for people dealing with affairs and asked that those interested in such a group call him. When they called, he gave them information about it and told them where to go for the first meeting; however, he did not attend the meetings or play any active role in them, since a support group consists only of those who have personally experienced this problem.

In each of these situations the people were able to make contact with others in a nonthreatening way in order to get the support groups organized. These are just a few ideas; there are surely many others.

Once you succeed in establishing a support group, it's important to recognize just what's involved and understand the role of the organizer. At the meetings themselves, the organizer is there to participate as a full member, not just to help others. It's their responsibility to share their feelings and experiences just as the others are to do. It's important that there are no experts and no leaders, so that each person is an equal member of the group and participates in such a way as to empower everyone present.

One important factor in the success of the meetings is that the organizer and the other participants agree to some basic guidelines for the group. Here are the guidelines for support groups that I laid out in *Beyond Affairs,* which formed the basis for the work I did with those who became members of BAN.

GUIDELINES FOR SUPPORT GROUPS

1. Be honest in your sharing. Avoid any tendency to "put up a good front." Don't compete by trying to sound better or worse off than someone else. Remember . . . you're all in this together and you don't have to impress anybody.

2. Support each other in feeling good about yourselves and your ability to cope with the situation. Self-confidence is vital in getting beyond the pain. This means not getting bogged down in "blaming" and griping about "how awful it is." Acknowledging these feelings may be necessary and useful, but going over and over them doesn't change anything—and may do you harm. It can keep you feeling sorry for yourself, and this just makes it harder to develop your sense of self-worth.

3. Really listen to the other people in your group. You've come together to support each other. That can't happen if you're only thinking about yourself.

4. Don't debate differences of opinion. Being supportive means avoiding "approving" or "disapproving." There's no need to be in agreement. Support comes from understanding and accepting—not from judging.

5. Avoid "leading" questions or "helpful" advice, such as:

"Why don't you . . . ?"

"Did you try . . . ?"

"I think you should . . ."

"If it were me, I'd . . ."

6. Ask clarifying questions to help each person think things through for themselves, such as:

"How long have you felt this way?"

"Have you discussed this with anyone else?"

"What have you tried?"

"What are your alternatives?"

7. Talk about your feelings. That's more important than the details of your experience.

8. If you feel angry—admit it. You can't overcome it as long as you hide or deny it. This doesn't mean you have to act on it. Just openly acknowledging your anger is the first step toward loosening its power.

9. If you feel guilty, say so. You may be holding secret fears that somehow it's all your fault. Again, you need to acknowledge the feelings before you can deal with them. There are many burdens of guilt you may have put on yourself that you need to get rid of. You could feel:

—guilty that you failed to have the "ideal" relationship.

—guilty that you're leaving your partner.

—guilty that you're not leaving your partner.

—guilty that you feel angry or vindictive.

10. Freely respond to others when they express feelings that you understand or can identify with. This may not seem very important, but it can be critical in giving them the strength they need and letting them see they're not alone. You can offer comments, such as:

"I know how you feel."

"I've had that experience, too."

"That's one of my concerns . . . or fears . . . or uncertainties."

11. Remember that the group cannot decide how you should feel or what you should do. It can provide support for you to figure things out for yourself.[1]

OTHER GROUPS
· · · · · · ·

The BAN Support Group on the Internet is the only national support group for dealing with affairs, but there are some other groups that might prove helpful. Simply participating in a support group, whatever the particular issue, can have some healing effect.

ALCOHOLICS ANONYMOUS

While it doesn't specifically deal with the issue of affairs, some people have found help by attending meetings of Alcoholics Anonymous or Al-Anon. For instance, one of the primary messages in Al-Anon is that the spouse of an alcoholic can't take responsibility for their partner's drinking. In the same way, the spouse of a person who had an affair can't take responsibility for their partner's affair.

Another concept in dealing with alcoholism is recognizing how the people around alcoholics actually make it easier for them to drink by covering up for them so they don't have to face the consequences of their alcoholism. For instance, one woman who was married to an alcoholic always tried to get him into bed and clean up the mess he made in the bathroom when he got sick from too much alcohol. In Al-Anon, she was encouraged to let her husband remain on the floor in his own vomit so he'd wake up and see where he was.

Similarly, the spouse of a person having an affair may know it's happening but turn the other way and not confront it, allowing the one having the affair to avoid facing the pain being caused by their behavior. And after confronting a mate's affair, a person often hides it from others; so the one who had the affair (like the alcoholic) never has to deal with the mess they have made.

SEXAHOLICS ANONYMOUS

This is a group that addresses the issue of affairs as a sexual addiction. A sex addict is defined as a person who is addicted to the sexual experience and its surrounding behaviors. This includes deviant sexual behavior that has nothing to do with affairs, and has been used to describe any person whose sex life is destructive and out of control. Unfortunately, many people are tempted to grasp at this simple explanation as the cause of affairs, whether or not it fits. Certainly there are sexual deviants in society, but considering the number of people having affairs, this is hardly "deviant" behavior. As we've seen from the statistics, it's actually the norm.

Despite major misgivings about inappropriately labeling someone who has affairs as a "sexaholic," if this is the only group support a person is willing to pursue, it may be better than none at all. The potential benefit would be from talking about this issue with others who have had similar experiences as a way of getting more perspective on the consequences of their own behavior. And, as with Al-Anon, there are also groups for spouses of "sexaholics."

MARRIAGE ENCOUNTER

This is another well-known group, though not an ongoing one like the ones mentioned above. It's a weekend experience for couples who want to improve their relationship, specifically their communication skills. Participation in this group does not involve sharing in the group as a whole. It's based on personal writing that is shared only with your partner.

Volunteer couples working with the organization serve as "presenters," sharing some issue in their own marriage as a catalyst for private discussions between the couples in attendance. In some instances, the sample issue may, in fact, be affairs. But regardless of the particular issue demonstrated, couples who attend may be helped by hearing how other couples communicate, thereby improving their own communication.

Marriage Encounter has traditionally been sponsored by religious organizations. Some people might think that any religious group or member of the clergy would take a stereotypically judgmental attitude toward this issue. While this is no doubt true in some cases, I've found some of the most thoughtful, compassionate, nonjudgmental people to be among the clergy. I was especially impressed with some of the support we received from them when we were promoting *Beyond Affairs*. In several cases, they were outspoken supporters of what we were doing and made use of the book in their work with couples, both individually and in groups.

There may be instances, of course, where a member of the clergy has no training in dealing with the issue of affairs. In fact, one woman wrote that her clergyman was very appreciative of her giving him a copy of our book because he acknowledged that he did not have a good understanding of this issue. But one of the benefits of working with one of the many members of the clergy who *are* skilled in this area is that in most cases it allows couples who might otherwise avoid professional help due to financial concerns to receive counseling.

BOOKS
• • • • • • •

Another source of help in dealing with the issue of affairs is the perspective that can be gained from books and other written materials. This, of course, can be in conjunction with whatever other help a person is receiving. There's a need to make use of every available source of help if a person is to make the best possible recovery from this experience.

One problem with books on this subject is that most of them are aimed *only* at women whose husbands have had affairs. Since women comprise the largest segment of the book-buying public, it's an understandable trend. But in addition to this, women tend to think that anything that goes wrong in their relationship is their fault. So if their partner has an affair, they're eager to find a book that will tell them what they did to cause it to happen and what they can do to keep it from happening again. Unfortunately, most of these books address women's insecurities and reinforce the view of women as the caretakers of the relationship.

Neither men nor women are well-served by the tone of most of the books dealing with affairs or other issues related to male-female relationships. Many of them show disdain for both men and women by focusing on who is to blame for whatever problems exist. But the overwhelming focus on men as the ones who have affairs (or who won't commit, or who can't love) leads to a "male-bashing" attitude that has many thoughtful people concerned.

It's gotten to be an unfunny joke to review the list of book titles with this theme: *Men Who Can't Be Faithful (How to Pick up the Pieces When He's Breaking Your Heart); Back from Betrayal (Recovering from His Affairs); How to Keep Your Man Monogamous; Men Who Can't Love; Men Who Hate Women and the Women Who Love Them; Cold Feet: Why Men Don't Commit; How to Keep a Man in Love with You Forever* . . .

Unfortunately, this trend reinforces the idea that any shortcomings in love, monogamy, or commitment are purely personal failures, mostly by men. If women are viewed as being at fault in any of these areas, it's more likely to be due to an *excess* of love or commitment, as in *Women Who Love Too Much.*

We need to get away from so much blaming and try to understand more about the conditioning that has led to the problems in male-female relationships. A person dealing with the issue of affairs can benefit significantly from learning more about the differences in the sexes and how they came about. Some books that offer insight into men and women's differences are *The Inner Male* by Herb Goldberg, *Femininity* by Susan Brownmiller, and *Male and Female Realities* by Joe Tanenbaum.

There are many books dealing with affairs and with developing good relationships between the sexes. But it's important to read a wide variety of books to get any real perspective on these issues, because no one book has all the answers and most books have a certain bias that would be balanced by reading others. Since almost every book contains *some* useful information and insights, I often feel a book is worthwhile if I get just one good idea from it. There's a bibliography at the back of this book that offers possibilities for further reading.

BECOMING YOUR OWN EXPERT
• • • • • • •

As we've seen, help in dealing with affairs is available in many ways for the person who wants it and is willing to seek it. By taking advantage of these resources, you can become your own expert on male-female relationships in general, as well as the specific issue of affairs. This is because the bottom line is finding what works for *you*. While there are no absolute answers to many of the questions about affairs, learning as much as possible about the issue can help piece together those answers that make sense on an individual basis.

The ability to gain this expertise depends on the attitude with which you approach it. If you're only trying to find reassurance or to prove some position or preconceived notion, you won't benefit in the way that's possible when the focus is to get information, understanding, and perspective. Too often, people take one book or one idea and try to make it fit every situation. Even worse for a relationship, one person may take the information they obtain and try to force it on their partner in a way that is sure to create defensiveness. You may be able to become your own expert, but you can't presume to be the expert for everyone else.

It's also important to avoid looking for a quick fix, since anything that is too simple will probably fail to provide the kind of long-lasting help you need. If you get confused by conflicting advice, just realize there are no "ultimate" answers; it's up to you to check within yourself to see what makes sense for your particular situation.

The final benefit of making an effort to get as much help as possible is not just for getting a better understanding of affairs or for achieving some peace of mind. It's also the best way to be prepared to make good decisions about the future, especially in resolving what for most people is the most critical issue—the marriage/divorce dilemma.

RESOURCES TO HELP YOU HELP YOURSELF
• • • • • • •

Some of the best resources for dealing with relationship issues can be found on the Internet. One such site is the Coalition for Marriage, Family and Couples Education (CMFCE). You can visit their Website (www.smartmarriages.com) or contact them at their offices in Washington, D.C., for information about courses and seminars offered around the country by the dozens of top professionals.

Our site (www.vaughan-vaughan.com) offers extensive information about affairs, as well as hosting a password-protected support group, Beyond Affairs Network (BAN), for men and women struggling to recover from a partner's affair. There is also a group for men and women who had an affair and want to save their marriage. While BAN provides support for saving marriages (or committed relationships), it also supports people's effort to recover from the emotional impact—regardless of whether the marriage survives.

One common problem faced by those who decide to stay with a spouse who has had an affair is that people often say, Why?—as if they *shouldn't* stay. Besides the practical reasons for staying, there are also some important reasons a person might *want* to stay: They may still love their spouse (despite the hurt and anger), they may value their shared history and their mutual goals, they may see hope for using this crisis to develop a better relationship than before, and they may decide that they prefer their spouse to either being alone or to other potential partners.

Of course, making the decision to try to save the marriage is only the first step. Rebuilding the trust that has been shattered by the affair depends on some basic behaviors on the part of the person who had the affair: being willing to answer your questions, hanging in while you deal with the understandable emotions, and demonstrating a commitment to the relationship by severing contact with the third party.

Without this kind of effort, the marriage is less likely to survive; or if it does, it may be a deadened, meaningless marriage. And even with this effort, it is likely to take several years to fully recover. While no one would choose to go through this ordeal, it's possible to develop a stronger relationship and greater trust than was possible with the "blind trust" that came from believing the Monogamy Myth. I'm not saying everyone *should* stay in their marriage. I am simply saying that we should respect and support each person's individual choices—even when we disagree or fail to understand.

PART IV

· · · · · · ·

A TIME OF RECKONING

9

·······

The Marriage/Divorce Dilemma

Since most people remain in a state of shock or emotional disorientation for some time after learning of a mate's affair, it's essential that they wait until their emotions are under better control before deciding the future of the relationship. The period immediately following their discovery is definitely not the time to make such a life-altering decision as to whether to stay married or get a divorce—most people are incapable of thinking clearly at this time.

For instance, one woman kept thinking of crazy things like, if she got a divorce and they sold the house, the dog would have to be put to sleep because you can't have dogs in apartments. She would get so upset by that fact that she couldn't get beyond it to even begin to cope with the possible effect on the children. A person in this state is clearly not prepared to make a rational decision about the future of their marriage.

AMBIVALENCE
······

When a person discovers their mate's affair, they're likely to go through a period of great ambivalence and uncertainty—when it's painful to look back and scary to look forward. While the question of whether to stay married or to get a divorce may dominate their thinking, they can't quite bring themselves to make a decision.

I'm not sure what to do, so I don't do anything. I don't want to appear desperate, so I don't attempt to contact her, yet I don't want to close the door, so I don't start divorce proceedings. Not a good place to be.

One of the reasons for the ambivalence about making this decision is because there's so much at stake. On the one hand, there's often a strong impulse to leave when a partner has an affair. But on the other hand, most people have invested themselves—their time, their energy, and their dreams—in this relationship, and they don't want to give it up without being sure they're not making a mistake. Even if the relationship is less than they had hoped, they see no guarantee of finding a better one to replace it. And, on a subconscious level, most people fear the unknown; so staying until they're sure about leaving seems the most reasonable thing to do.

This ambivalence is not necessarily bad; in fact, it's preferable to the impulse to decide too quickly. Any hasty decisions are likely to complicate the difficult process of coping with the aftermath of an affair. A person who takes time to recover some sense of emotional stability before deciding their future will be more likely to make a satisfying decision.

Of couse, it's extremely difficult to cope with this period of uncertainty; until the decision is made, a person is likely to be completely preoccupied with the question of whether to stay or to leave. One BAN member found help and solace during this time of deliberation from the book *How to Survive the Loss of a Love*. She used the first three lines of one of the poems in the book and adapted the rest of the poem to express her own struggle with this dilemma.

"to give you up.
God!
What a bell of freedom that rings within me"[1]
no more wanting to understand what makes you tick
no more wanting to be able to communicate freely
no more waiting for reassurance, for explanation,
    or words that never come
no more wondering what you are doing

or who you are with
and then
no more depression
and FINALLY
no more hurting
and all it would take
    is to give you up
but that
    would take too much.

Sometimes a person gets so tired of trying to figure out what to do that they wish someone else would make the decision for them. I remember a period when I was so tired of trying to cope with my emotions that even though I wasn't willing to make the decision to leave, I thought James might get so tired of dealing with all my questions that *he* would decide to end the marriage. I came to the point of wishing someone else could make the decision for me. I just didn't feel like continuing to struggle with it. Fortunately, James was able to continue talking with me and supporting my efforts to understand and to overcome my emotions until I was finally clear that I wanted to stay.

A joint effort in deciding the future of a relationship can improve the chances of making a good decision. But all too often, the spouse who had an affair is unwilling to participate in this effort.

I feel that I am forced to be the stabilizing force; I do not feel that any plans are being formulated together. I am very resentful that I am the one who is left to labor over how to get things right—that I seem to have to carry the burden for finding solutions—when his actions are the ones that upset the applecart.

This failure of the spouse who had an affair to cooperate in the decision usually increases the frustration and resentment of the person who is trying to deal with their feelings about the affair. And it also contributes to their ambivalence about whether or not they want to save the marriage.

THE SPOUSE'S AMBIVALENCE

Ironically, the spouse's behavior may also be motivated by feelings of ambivalence. In the upheaval following the discovery of an affair, the person who had the affair often feels uncertain of their own feelings about the marriage. While they may not decide to leave, they may not invest any energy in improving the relationship either. When it's the wife who had an affair, she may resign herself to the idea of staying because of a fear of not being able to make it on her own financially. She may see it as the "lesser of two evils."

When it's the husband who had an affair, he sometimes has a similar ambivalence. Contrary to popular belief, men have a strong nesting instinct in that they want a home base (of whatever kind) rather than being alone. Most men don't leave a marriage unless they're clear about wanting to pair up with another woman. Just as with the woman who has an affair and stays in the marriage for "convenience," a man who has an affair may choose to do the same. Unfortunately, neither of them is likely to put much effort into making the marriage more than a practical base from which to pursue their individual lives.

Another common problem is that the person who has an affair sometimes doesn't know what they want. (They may not want a divorce but they may not want to give up the affair either.) For some people, the spouse's unwillingness to give up the affair is seen as a sign that the marriage is not salvageable, and this precipitates their decision to leave. But for the person who still wants to try to rebuild the marriage, this creates quite a challenge.

If they decide to give their mate some time to end the affair, they need to establish a time frame within which this action is to take place. While it's not a matter of giving an ultimatum per se, it's probably wise to establish an expectation of when this is to happen; otherwise, there may be an endless series of promises and procrastinations. Most people who are still involved in an affair after their mate knows about it are simply thinking for the moment and ignoring the need to choose between the marriage and the affair. This often continues until a decision is demanded, either by their mate or by their lover.

So each person must decide for themselves how long they are

willing to wait for their spouse to end the affair and begin working on the marriage. They need to be sure of their commitment to whatever deadline they set before clearly conveying that information to their spouse. Then, of course, they need to act in accordance with their decision.

It often becomes extremely difficult for a person who is waiting out their spouse's decision about ending the affair to think clearly in the midst of such conflicting feelings, but thinking is exactly what is needed. And the difficulty becomes even greater when it involves resisting the pressure of others as to what decision *they* think is best.

ADVICE FROM OTHERS

The advice from others usually falls into two broad categories: those who say to "forgive and forget" and those who say to "kick the bum/slut" out. Those who point out that the marriage vows say "for better or for worse" usually think a person should try to save the marriage at all costs. While this is a nice sentiment, it ignores the lasting impact this experience has on most people. It's certainly possible for a person to eventually put this behind them, but it's neither reasonable nor desirable to try to bury reality under a platitude without dealing with the situation and their feelings about it.

There are other people who are just as adamant in their opinion that the person who had an affair should not be forgiven and that the marriage should end *immediately*. People who hold this attitude feel very strongly that the person who had an affair should be punished. Unfortunately, this self-righteous attitude ignores the impact on the person who is to do the punishing. It's always easier for people to be arbitrary and rigid when they don't personally have to deal with the consequences. For the person who must make the decision, there is much to consider in deciding whether to stay or to leave.

In the final analysis, each person is responsible for making their own decision (regardless of the opinions of friends, family, professionals, or the general public) because they have to live with the choice they make. It takes strength and clearheadedness for a person to independently assess the situation and do whatever is best for them. They need to avoid making a decision purely on emotion; it's critical that they be able to think through all the factors, both emotional and practical.

THE PRACTICAL FACTORS
· · · · · · ·

Some people are critical of the idea of considering practical factors in deciding whether to stay married or get a divorce. They have the sense that a person should stick to certain principles, no matter what the cost. But those people are usually the ones who haven't personally faced this dilemma.

MONEY

Concerns about money are usually critical for a person who is contemplating divorce (whether it's the one who had an affair or the spouse who discovered their mate's affair). We tend to think that money is a serious consideration only for women considering divorce—that men don't let it stand in the way. We have also assumed that a man who discovers his wife's affair is more likely to get a divorce than a woman who discovers her husband's affair, but this is by no means clear. Our stereotypical thinking about a man being more likely to get a divorce has ignored the extent to which money considerations affect his decision as well.

Studies have shown that men's standard of living tends to improve following divorce. Since most men don't have enough money to be able to support two separate households in keeping with their previous standard of living, those who improve their own standard of living usually do so at the expense of their ex-wife and children. But a man who is committed to contributing to child support knows he's unlikely to be able to maintain the same lifestyle if he gets a divorce and establishes a separate residence, so he may find it very difficult to make a decision that he knows will lower his standard of living. Husbands in this position (who would otherwise choose to leave) may look at the prospect of the financial drain of divorce, and decide to stay in the marriage.

Although a man may feel trapped by the situation, he may resign himself to staying until the kids are grown. This hope for a future time when he may be able to make a different decision can make it easier for him to cope with the immediate decision based on the practical problem of money.

The significance of money considerations is even greater for most women who are considering divorce—and with good reason. A woman who gets a divorce (especially if there are children involved) often finds that her standard of living drops dramatically. According to the work of Lenore Weitzman reported in *The Divorce Revolution*, the decline in the standard of living for women with minor children during the first year following divorce is 73 percent on average.

A common situation for women who have never worked outside the home (or haven't worked in many years) is to wonder how they can pay their bills if they get a divorce. However, money is a major concern for women who are employed as well—since the income-earning potential of women is still much lower than that of men.

Just as with the man who makes a decision based on money, many wives who feel unprepared to support themselves and their children decide to stay in a marriage they would otherwise choose to leave. While a woman may feel at a given point that she has no other choice but to stay in the marriage, it doesn't mean she must continue that way forever. The time can be used to learn a skill or to build confidence or whatever it takes to become able to make it on her own, if that's what she wants to do. It's important that she work toward what she wants, whether or not she can have it immediately. The thing that can break her spirit is not just feeling that she has no choice *now*, but feeling she will *never* have a choice.

One woman who felt unsure of her ability to make it on her own decided to stay in the marriage while she went back to school. She studied business, with an eye toward eventually starting her own small company. Besides preparing her to face life in a practical way, her experience also provided her with much-needed confidence. By the time she felt secure enough to get a divorce, her relationship with her husband had improved to the point that she decided to stay in the marriage after all.

Child Support Payments

Concerns about basic income are not the only financial factors that need to be considered when thinking of divorce. If there are children, one of the biggest questions is how much child support will be awarded and how much will actually get paid—and for how long. Since it's usually the man who is charged with paying child support, his execution of this responsibility makes it extremely difficult for him to afford to remarry and establish another family. On the other hand, failure to receive child support leaves many women living at or below the poverty level.

Child-care Costs

Another money-related issue that must be considered is the cost of child care. Since custody is still usually granted to the mother, a woman's primary problem may be how to afford child care while she works. If she has already been working outside the home and has established child-care services, these are likely to be unaffordable with a reduced income. And if she has been a full-time home-maker caring for the children at home, she may feel overwhelmed by the dual challenge of finding and affording reliable child care.

One woman (who was in serious financial stress following her divorce) was able to find another divorced woman and child to share a house with her and her young daughter. Together the women operated a day-care center in their home as a means of making money while attending to their own child-care needs. While a woman may be able to find such creative ways to manage child care, there are other financial problems that create a much greater challenge. The reduction in family income experienced by most women after divorce is often compounded by the loss of other critical financial supports.

Other Financial Considerations

A major financial problem for a woman following divorce is the loss of medical benefits tied to her husband's employment. Lack of medical insurance coverage quickly becomes a nightmare (even if the father temporarily continues to provide coverage for the children). She is faced with the problem of paying any deductibles (or other health-care costs for the children not covered by the father's insurance), as well as her own health-care costs. It can be financially devastating for a woman to need hospital care (even for a couple of days) prior to establishing her own medical insurance coverage. Women in this position have been known to forego needed treatment or to begrudgingly turn to family members for financial help.

Another less immediate (but equally serious) financial problem is a woman's loss of access to her husband's pension benefits, creating a bleak future for her later years. Whereas a man's money concerns may complicate his decision to remarry, the money problems felt by a woman following divorce often lead her to remarry as quickly as possible to cope with a situation she sees no other way to resolve.

CHILDREN

As we've seen, when considering divorce, concerns about money are often intertwined with concerns about the children's welfare. While the combined problem of children and money often causes people to decide they must stay in the marriage, sometimes it leads to a very different kind of decision. For instance, one woman decided that the strain between her and her husband made life too difficult for the children if they continued to stay together. But she believed that if she got a divorce and had custody of the children, her husband would not freely contribute to the children's financial needs or fully participate in their lives. She knew that she couldn't provide the kind of life she wanted for the children; so after much soul-searching, she decided to give custody to her husband. This decision was criticized by others in her family, but she felt clear about her motives in making it; and she was committed to remaining a part of the children's lives, no matter how difficult it might be.

Having custody of the children can be a tremendous challenge for a man in that he is probably assuming a degree of responsibility that he has not previously held—taking care of the children while continuing to handle the normal requirements of his job. Some couples, of course, are able to develop a plan for sharing custody (which is usually designed to be most beneficial to the children), but there are problems connected with *any* arrangement. That's because the particular arrangement is not as critical as the attitude of the parents in carrying it out. Sometimes the animosity between the parents during the years following a divorce creates a constant state of stress and tension for the children, who often become pawns in their parents' struggle for power and influence.

One woman candidly described how her decision *not* to get a divorce was based on the fact that she knew her husband would continue to be a part of her life because he was the children's father. And the prospect of dealing with him under those circumstances seemed even more difficult than the idea of trying to work things out and stay married. Fortunately, he was equally committed to the children, and together they were able to work on their relationship and develop a marriage that was not only good for the children, but satisfying for them as well.

It's not unusual for people to decide to stay married "for the sake of the children." While we often think of mothers making this decision, it's equally true for fathers who fear they may lose their children forever if they get a divorce. Staying together for the sake of the children is a time-honored idea that has come to be questioned in recent years. Divorce has become so common that we've tended to think children cope with divorce much better today than in times past. But *Second Chances*, Judith S. Wallerstein's report on her ten-year follow-up study of families of divorce, indicates that the negative impact of divorce on children may be greater than we thought.

Wallerstein's most startling finding is that while we have viewed the trauma of divorce as a short-term one, it appears to have a long-lasting impact on children. Ten years following the divorce of their parents, she found that the divorce continued to be a major factor in the lives of the children (who were now between eleven and twenty-nine years old). Her conclusion from the interviews: "Life has been far more difficult than most imagined it would be."[2]

This new data does not mean it's best to avoid divorce at all costs, since some of the children did quite well following the divorce of their parents. The critical message is the importance of the way parents handle the divorce and their relationship with the children during the intervening years. Despite the difficulties of divorce for everyone involved, including the children, Wallerstein puts it in perspective: "To recognize that divorce is an arduous, long-lasting family trauma is not to argue against it. Divorce is a useful and necessary social remedy. And the fact is that most divorces with children are not impulsive. . . . Most worry about the effects of divorce on their children. There is considerable evidence that a conflict-ridden marriage is not in the best interests of the children. There is evidence, too, that children benefit from dissolution of such marriages."[3]

One of the ways divorce can have a negative impact on children is when one of the parents in essence becomes an absentee parent. In the case of an extramarital affair, this is often the parent involved in the affair. Occasionally, the person having an affair becomes so absorbed by their outside relationship that they cease to care about anything else, including the children. This presents an exceptionally difficult situation for the spouse. They are placed in the position of dealing with their own feelings of rejection while attending to their children's sense of rejection by the other parent.

One man (who had moved in with the other woman) seemed to deliberately avoid contact with his children. It was as if they were a reminder of a life he wanted to forget. He seemed oblivious to their feelings, never calling or initiating any contact. The only time he saw them was when he occasionally needed to stop by the house to get something or to handle some legal matter related to the pending divorce. While their mother was suffering her own sense of rejection, it was still outweighed by her concern about the children. She tried to pretend their father was busy and didn't have time to spend with them, but the children were old enough and perceptive enough to question this explanation. So she finally realized it was better to go ahead and tell them the truth.

Telling the Children

When a parent moves out of the house to be with their lover, telling the children may be unavoidable; but it's usually a real dilemma as to whether or not to tell the kids about a parent's affair. There is, of course, no absolute answer. It depends on the children's ages, their maturity, and how perceptive they are of what's going on around them. Most children are far more aware than we realize, and the conflict between what they see on the outside and what they sense on the inside can create special problems for them. A child who knows something is wrong (but doesn't know what) may deal better with facts than with fears. In the absence of knowing the source of a problem, kids have a strong tendency to assume the problem has to do with them—that whatever is wrong is somehow their fault.

Perhaps the more important consideration as to whether or not it's a good idea to talk to the kids about these issues is to consider the attitude with which the information is related to them. This will greatly affect the way in which they hear it and deal with it. If they feel they're having a huge burden of anger and resentment laid on them, then they're likely to have a hard time dealing with it. But if they can be given the information (including information about the feelings, but not *demonstrations* of the feelings), then they are likely to be able to hear it and deal with it in a way that can help them make sense of what's going on around them.

Ideally, both the mother and father would be present when telling the children, and they would have agreed in advance about what is to be said. It's important to let the children know that this is the parents' problem, not theirs. The children need to be reassured that it has nothing to do with them and to be told that both parents love them very much. And, finally, they need to be told that the parents are trying to work it out (if that's the case) or to be told of any plans for separation or divorce if that is the next step.

Our kids were eleven and thirteen when we told them about James's affairs. We felt good about our decision at the time, but it was even more valuable in serving as a basis for our ongoing honest communication with them about issues related to sex and marriage. For instance, when discussing marriage with our daughter several years before her own marriage, we tried to convey some of our understandings about the difficulty in developing a good marriage. We were concerned that she discounted many of the potential problems by thinking (like I and many others) that "my marriage will be different." I knew it could be different, but only if both she and her husband made a conscious effort to make it different. She now understands that monogamy can't be assumed; it must be achieved by a commitment to honesty and an effort to communicate feelings on an ongoing basis.

But it isn't just the problems of divorce or affairs that we discuss with our kids; it's the overall quality of the marital relationship. Our son, who is not married, is very thoughtful about the need to delay marriage until he feels prepared to give it the kind of energy and commitment required to have a good relationship. He sees the importance of knowing who he is as a person before undertaking the kind of sharing and understanding called for by marriage and a family. This makes us hopeful that he will succeed in avoiding the plight that befalls so many marriages.

OTHER PRACTICAL CONSIDERATIONS

While money and kids are the most significant practical considerations in trying to decide whether to stay married or get a divorce, they're not the only ones. There's a wide range of factors that are important to different people: involvement with a home or garden, being in business together and not wanting to lose what they've worked for, elderly parents who would be hurt by their divorce, and (perhaps the most common concern) the impact on their relationships with friends and other family members.

Concern about the reaction of family members (especially if they disapprove of a particular decision) often becomes a real barrier to thinking clearly about whether to stay or leave. Unfortunately, regardless of the circumstances leading up to the decision, a person who decides to get a divorce frequently feels they are "blamed" for the failure of the marriage.

Most people realize there will be changes in their family relationships after a divorce, but they're seldom prepared for just how alienated some parts of the family may become. Staying in touch with a spouse's family when the divorce is the result of an affair can be exceptionally difficult. And if contact is maintained (perhaps because of the children), it may be quite strained and uncomfortable for all concerned. Some people make the mistake of trying to force new patterns of family interactions too quickly following a divorce, when everyone is still trying to adjust to the situation. But being patient and taking things one day at a time makes it more tolerable in the short term, as well as more likely that it will become easier with the passage of time.

There's another important consideration for the person trying to make a decision about marriage vs. divorce: An emotional issue like affairs often alienates family members from *both* of the people involved, regardless of whether they stay married or get a divorce. It's understandable that the relatives of the person who did not have the affair may align themselves with that person, but their intense criticism and hostility toward the spouse who had an affair may add to the turmoil of the situation. Surprisingly, the relatives of the person who did have an affair may avoid contact with the one who didn't have an affair—usually based on their discomfort with the whole situation and the tendency in society to suppress open discussion of affairs. It will help to acknowledge in advance that some valued family relationships will be damaged, and to be prepared to work to gradually improve them.

A divorce also frequently causes major changes in friends and social life. People who were mutual friends may try to stay neutral in the beginning, but their feelings of awkwardness often lead them to "choose sides" and continue the friendship with only one member of the couple. In other cases, friends who were strictly "couple friends" (part of a network of couples who were social friends but not friends on an individual basis) may avoid further contact with *both* of the people involved, simply because they're no longer a couple.

It's not unusual for a person to find themselves losing contact with all the old friends who were "our" friends, but that's not necessarily bad. While the changes in relationships following a divorce may feel entirely negative, there's sometimes a beneficial result to the changes. For instance, it's possible to find out who your "real" friends are and to develop friendships based on more depth and substance than was formerly the case. It's also possible to look back on friendships that have ended and see that they were destructive in that they stifled your growth as a person and your sense of what you could do in life. And it offers the possibility of developing new friends who stimulate your thinking and your interest in new and different areas. As with almost every facet of dealing with the issue of affairs, there's a potential negative and a potential positive effect from either a decision to stay married or a decision to get a divorce.

While some particular practical problem may be so overriding that it becomes the determining factor in a person's final decision, most people will find it necessary to sort through all the various considerations before coming to a conclusion as to whether to stay or to leave. There is no simple formula for making such a complex decision, but a review of some of the key points in the process may lead to greater satisfaction with whatever choice is made.

SOME GUIDELINES FOR SOLVING THE MARRIAGE/DIVORCE DILEMMA
• • • • • • •

1. Make your *own* decision (regardless of what others think).
2. Do not rush the decision.
3. Get as much information as possible about your own situation and about affairs in general.
4. Consider the emotional aspect of this, but realize it's only one part, not the sole basis for a good decision.
5. Consider the practical factors involved (including money, kids, and other relevant issues), but realize the importance of balancing these concerns with the more personal, emotional needs.
6. Base the decision not just on the past, but on the future. No one has a crystal ball to see just what the future holds, but there are indications that can serve as a guide:

- Is there a willingness to talk about what happened and to try to learn from it?
- Is there a willingness to use the information in a constructive way instead of using it as a way to punish past behavior?
- Is there a willingness to acknowledge attractions as normal and likely in the future, and a plan for ongoing discussions of these temptations?

- Is there a commitment to honesty as the basis of the relationship (rather than just a promise of monogamy)?
- Is there evidence of a willingness to be honest by ongoing sharing of thoughts and feelings about subjects other than affairs? (If there is not honest communication about other issues, there's little likelihood there will be honesty in talking about affairs.)
- Even if there's no evidence of the things listed above *at this time*, does it seem reasonable to think of moving *toward* this way of relating? Changes of this kind don't happen overnight, but unless there's an indication of movement in this direction, there's little hope for developing a good marriage.

Deciding whether to stay married or get a divorce is a complicated decision, but carefully considering all these factors can help a person sort through their personal values and priorities to make the decision that best fits their individual situation. And by making a decision in a rational way (instead of reacting to the panic of the initial shock of the affair or to the pressure from others to decide more quickly), they should reap the benefits of being better prepared to live with whatever decision they make.

10
· · · · · · ·

Living with the Decision

There isn't any right or wrong decision to make about staying married or getting a divorce, only the one that works for each individual personally. Two different people may have the same set of conditions but make different decisions—and in each case it might be the best decision for each of them. That's because people have differing values and priorities about factors that have an impact on their decision.

For instance, two men who are considering divorce might each have the same income and the same number of children and other family responsibilities; but one might choose to stay in the marriage and one decide to leave. One man may value his life with his children above all else, whereas another man may never have felt very comfortable with his role as a father and have no problem adjusting to the idea of not living with his kids. As to money, one man may value a more luxurious lifestyle and be unwilling to shift to the lower standard of living a divorce would bring, whereas another man may be very "basic" and prefer the simple life without regard to outward appearances. Whatever a person's decision, we need to respect it and respect them for having the courage to make it.

CHOOSING TO STAY
· · · · · · ·

Most people who decide to stay in the marriage feel that in order to rebuild the marriage they must be able to forgive their spouse for having an affair. But as long as an affair continues to be seen only in personal terms (as something one person does *to* another), true forgiveness is unlikely. This is why it's so important to understand an individual's actions in terms of how the larger environment impacts on their values—and how those values can change over time.

For instance, my husband was monogamous for the first eleven years of our marriage; but through the years, as he became exposed to other people and other ideas, he began to change his way of thinking. When he had his first affair he had not actually *decided* in advance. But by the time it happened, his new attitudes had led him to be ready when the opportunity arose. I'm not saying that society or his peers were responsible for his actions, only that he did not come to this point in isolation.

If a person decides to stay in the marriage, it's important that they consider whether they are able to view their spouse's behavior in this larger perspective. By not feeling there's been a personal assault that requires forgiveness, it becomes much easier to deal with the next major challenge for the person who decides to stay in the marriage—to feel loving and giving again.

Nothing positive that I said or did made any difference. (For the record, and he will be the first to admit it, I have always built up his self-esteem, been interested in him and his work, waited on him, bought little "I love you" presents, sent cards for no occasions, and all the things that loving people do.) It's not like I never did these things until after his affair. Now I'm so tempted to be the reverse type of wife—I mean, where did the other way get me?

It's quite understandable that the little loving actions and gestures that once seemed so natural may seem somewhat awkward for a while. But once the pain begins to subside, most people can usually return to doing these loving things. If, however, a person tries to be nice only in order to make a certain impression or get a certain reaction, then it's likely to backfire—most people can sense whether these actions are genuine or whether their partner is just trying to please out of a sense of insecurity. One is seen as giving and the other as begging.

If the genuine desire to be loving and caring doesn't return at some point, it's important to ask whether a person still has any love for their spouse, or whether they just want their spouse to love *them*. After feeling rejected by a spouse's affair, there's sometimes a strong need to feel wanted and desired again.

While this can happen with either men or women, it's especially true for women who have been conditioned to define themselves in terms of their ability to attract the opposite sex. This leads many women to focus more on being loved than on loving. Despite the popularity of the idea that women love too much, often it's not that they *love* too much, it's that they *want* to be loved too much. A common problem for many of us, whether male or female, is feeling "you're nobody 'til somebody loves you."

I'd be remiss if I didn't say a little more about the importance of another aspect of love that tends to get overlooked in the midst of this time of hurt and alienation. That is the real, honest-to-goodness physical attraction, the chemistry, that presumably once existed. If, before this crisis period, a person's heart "fluttered" and they felt "turned on" simply by seeing their mate again after a brief absence, then they have a much better chance of recovering from this experience. If this spark was already gone, the effort to recover the deeper loving feelings may be an overwhelming task.

There's a tendency to discount the importance of this basic attraction after years of developing a more comprehensive kind of love, but it shouldn't be underestimated in how much it may affect the chances for renewing the vitality of the marriage. I believe that an important part of my gut-level desire to stay married was that I never lost that special spark. Despite all that had happened, I was still *in love* with my husband. And it made all the difference.

DEALING WITH OTHERS' REACTIONS

Many people think that staying married after a spouse's affair is a sign of weakness and cowardice. While friends might not say it to your face, others can be quite blunt in their assessment of your decision. For instance, as a guest on a television talk show, I recall feeling the animosity of those in the audience who were quite distressed that I had stayed in the marriage after discovering my husband's affairs. One woman said, "I could understand it if he had had only *one* affair, but there's no excuse for putting up with so many." And another said, "I think you must be a weak person for not being able to get out of the marriage."

It was not, however, just some members of studio audiences who criticized my decision to stay in the marriage. In two instances when celebrity panelists were involved in the interviews, they expressed this same kind of irritation that I hadn't gotten a divorce. On "To Tell the Truth," one of the panelists said she would have left her husband if he had had an affair and was disappointed that I hadn't left mine. And one of the panelists on "Leave It to the Women" was even more extreme in her reaction. She said if he had been *her* husband she would have cut his "you know what" off with a meat axe.

At first glance, it might seem strange that people are so concerned about what decision another person makes. But their desire to see the person who has an affair punished is in part a reflection of their own personal fears about this issue. Somehow, they hope that if those who do it are punished, it will act as a deterrent to others (including their own partner). So they want me and others in my position to act on their behalf, to somehow protect them from having to deal with the issue themselves.

Of course, this attitude of wanting to punish the person who has an affair is another result of the view of affairs as a personal failure. By seeing affairs this way, people are able to separate themselves from the problem when it happens to others and stand in judgment of them personally. And their criticism of the person who stays married following a spouse's affair is also based on personal blame. A less personal interpretation of affairs would substantially lessen the problems for a person who decides to stay in the marriage, because they wouldn't be subjected to such overwhelmingly negative reactions from others for making this decision.

Another reason people are so critical of a person who stays married after a mate's affair is because they think *they* would have gotten a divorce. Of course, it's a fallacy for anyone to think they know how they would act if it happened to them, and it's even more unreasonable to think they know what's best for someone else. Unfortunately, people simply don't understand much about this issue unless they've been through it themselves. It's important for the person who decides to stay married to keep this perspective when confronted with the negative reactions of others.

CHOOSING TO LEAVE
· · · · · · ·

I do know at this point in my life divorce was the thing for me. I still love her and feel lonely at times, but these are all things I can handle. Being out of control of my life was intolerable.

There will be a sad divorce next week. I don't know if these things are ever right or wrong, but I feel to protect myself I have to move away—emotionally, perhaps physically.

Sometimes divorce is the only reasonable decision, but people seldom come to this conclusion easily. There's frequently a long period of deliberation, and that's as it should be; it takes time to get beyond the emotions to a point of being able to think clearly enough to make a good decision.

THE IMPORTANCE OF TIMING

Timing is one of the most crucial factors in determining the ability to live comfortably with the decision to get a divorce. If a person leaves too soon, the issues may never be fully dealt with. While the decision itself may not be wrong, there's a good possibility that making the decision before getting an understanding of what happened will leave unresolved feelings of bitterness and resentment. There may be unanswered questions and unspoken feelings that persist for years to come. Also, the impulse to leave immediately is often a reaction to the shock of a situation for which they're unprepared.

But delaying the decision too long is also likely to create lasting problems. While waiting long enough to overcome the initial shock of the affair is a positive step, it's important that the time be spent actually working toward making a decision rather than becoming trapped in a strained relationship simply by failing to decide. At some point, a person may know within their heart that it's time to leave, but continue to put off the actual departure. Then they discover that they've accommodated to a situation that would have seemed intolerable had they not waited so long that it became tolerable by virtue of its familiarity.

In some sense, there's a "window," a period of time when it's best to leave. Having missed the prime opening, some people feel the window is forever closed. As the crisis abates and they turn their attention to other areas of life, they simply give up the idea of leaving. It's sad when people give up on a relationshp too soon, but it's just as sad when they fail to leave an unrecoverable relationship.

There's no better way to illustrate the importance of "knowing when to leave" than to follow the thought processes of one woman who dealt with this dilemma. I first met her seven years ago, shortly after her separation from her husband, and we have continued our contact since that time. This is how she described her experience.

Initial contact:

> *I recently separated from my husband as a result of a relationship he has been having with another woman for the past year and a half. My close friends and family are very biased against him, and they all think I am crazy for not divorcing him right away.*

Two months later:

> *Whereas before, because of my own pride, I thought divorce was the only alternative, now I feel myself slowly opening up to the possibility that perhaps this relationship can survive. Or, at the very least, we can come to an understanding of how and why we came to where we are in our lives and not drag the pain and fears on into the future. At this point we are completely separated. I still love him and I miss him like crazy but I am unable to show or tell much about my true feelings. What a hellish way to be.*

Two months later:

> *My separation remains that. I have acquired a divorced woman and her child as roommates. I am still unemployed and that fact is more depressing than anything else. My husband and I continue to see each other but at times I feel nothing is really changing or happening with the relationship. But the thought of reconciliation at this point would not be good for either of us.*

Three months later:

> *We are filing for divorce this week. Both of us feel the need for things to be more finalized now and we are doing the divorce ourselves. We talk quite frequently about the situation and we share equally in parenting our child.*

Five months later:

> *My divorce is now final. I have been working full time for the past two months . . . a very rewarding but demanding job. I have a nice relationship going. My relationship with my ex is very good, and we share parenting with ease.*

Two years later:

> *I am happy to report that I share an unusual and quite rewarding relationship with a man who lives a little distance away. We have slowly worked at making the relationship fit us both over a period of two years. We have come to be very good friends and the trust factor is very present.*

Two years later:

> *I continue to participate in a very unique relationship. It's been four years and monogamy evolved naturally. Communication has been an important part of our relationship.*

Two years later:

My last name is different now. I married the man with whom I've had the six-year relationship. We are extremely happy and grateful for the time we took in considering this marriage. My husband threw a "This Is Your Life" birthday-roast for me, including many people from my past . . . even my ex-spouse. It was truly a wonderful event. Life is good and the future looks promising.

By looking at the way things developed over a seven-year period, it's clear that the eventual outcome depended both on timing and on patience in allowing herself to grow into a new life, going through the steps of pain and growth required to reach that point. Had she left immediately when pressured by her friends and family, or had she waited long past the time when it seemed right for both of them, they might not have had the kind of sensible, satisfying parting that actually took place. And they probably would not have had the kind of comfortable postmarital relationship they were able to develop (both for their own benefit and for that of their child), as indicated by the following reflection.

My ex-husband and I are fortunate in that we have been able to set aside our past and focus on making a joint-custody arrangement work. It has been working for several years now, and barring unforeseen circumstances, we look forward to a relatively smooth future.

WHEN IS THE TIME RIGHT?

The clearest guideline in considering the right time to leave was well stated above: ". . . at the very least, [when] we can come to an understanding of how and why we came to where we are in our lives and not drag the pain and fears on into the future." Unfortunately, it's not always easy to determine when a couple has come to this point.

For instance, one couple thought they had reached an impasse in their efforts to get beyond the negative feelings about the affair and agree on the kind of relationship they wanted to develop, so they decided on a trial separation of six months. After only three months of separation, they had gained additional insights into themselves and a new appreciation for the history they shared, leading them to decide to get back together. A year following that time they reported that their love was greater than it had ever been, with much better communication and honesty. Keeping a degree of openness about the decision, regardless of which decision is tentatively determined, can lead to finding the right time to leave (or finding that it isn't right to leave at all).

WHEN SOMEONE ELSE MAKES THE CHOICE

Sometimes a person doesn't make the choice to leave. Their spouse is the one who decides to end the marriage. In fact, it's not uncommon for a woman to learn only *after* her husband leaves that he had been having an affair. And in some cases, she might never have known except that he moved in with the other woman before the divorce was final. This can be a very difficult and embarrassing situation.

In one instance, what made it even more difficult was that the man married the other woman as soon as the divorce was final, and his children participated in the wedding. His ex-wife found this almost unbearable, but the children were teenagers and she felt they had the right to make their own decision. Her husband was marrying a woman not much older than their children, a woman who had small children of her own. The idea that her husband was abandoning his own family to raise someone else's children was the most painful part of the entire experience for her.

This particular woman's reaction was to question the very idea of marriage. In looking back at her own marriage, she felt she had been stupid to let her whole life revolve around her husband and family. But she wasn't stupid; she simply grew up in another generation, one that believed the woman's place was in the home taking care of the children. At the time she got married, most women didn't know they had a choice. Fortunately, young women today realize the importance of having their own interests in life and having a profession of their own. Hopefully, they will be able to avoid rejecting the idea of marriage if they have a marriage that ends in divorce.

But the bitterness about marriage expressed by some women of an earlier generation relates more to their idealistic expectations of marriage than to their frustrations about their role in the marriage. Even women who did not devote themselves exclusively to their role as wife and mother often felt this kind of disenchantment with marriage. A striking case is that of Patricia Neal, the Academy Award-winning actress.

Her reaction to the end of her marriage is even more powerful in light of the many tragedies she has faced in her life. In 1960 her young son was hit by a taxi in New York and survived with mild brain damage. Later, she lost a daughter to measles. In 1965, while pregnant with her fifth child, she suffered a series of strokes that left her in a coma for two weeks and threatened to permanently destroy her powers of speech. She miraculously recovered to a great extent following a long, difficult period of rehabilitation. But according to her, the blow that almost did her in was the breakup of her marriage, at her husband's instigation, when he left her for another woman: "So many horrendous things have happened to me, but I think the fact that our marriage has not worked is the most agonizing. I just can't swallow it. It's as if the worst dream I can think of has happened. This whole thing has been agonizing to me as a woman, and it's damaged my self-confidence. Life can be tough, it really can, and I don't know what tomorrow's going to be like. I do know I never want to be married again, ever."

There are no simple platitudes for dealing with the devastation of this experience, but life does go on and people do usually soften their negative attitudes about love and marriage. This can be seen in some of Patricia Neal's reflections during the five-year period following her divorce: "I do still have faith in life. And I do still believe in love."[1]

ADJUSTING TO DIVORCE
· · · · · · ·

The next major challenge for those who decide to get a divorce is adjusting to the changes in their lives that divorce inevitably brings. One woman (who expected to be relieved when she finalized a very messy divorce that had taken almost two years) found that she couldn't bring herself to get out of the house for a week. She took a week off from work and spent the time sleeping and watching old movies on television. Suddenly, the focus for her time and energy for the past two years was over. She hadn't realized it had so dominated her life that she was actually lost without that process to worry about. Strange, yet understandable stuff for anyone who has been through it.

Once a person recovers from the emotional shock of a divorce, the practical problems involved in getting resettled and establishing a new life pattern dominate a lot of their time and energy. While it's difficult to cope with the many serious adjustments to be made (like deciding where to live, handling job and money decisions, dealing with the impact of the divorce on the children), it's the seemingly inconsequential ones that sometimes feel overwhelming.

For instance, one problem peculiar to women is adjusting to the impact of divorce on their name (or their sense of who they are). One woman described how the dumbest things can get you down, like having to throw away a whole box of stationery imprinted with "Mrs. So & So." She even wondered if she would have to give it back if she won a sweepstakes prize as "Mrs. So & So."

FILLING TIME

To the surprise of many people, how to fill their time often becomes a particularly challenging aspect of the adjustment to a divorce. Everyone develops habits of structuring time in certain ways, usually built around their primary relationship. If that relationship ends, it calls for a complete restructuring of the way they spend their time.

I'm living alone for the first time in my entire life, and it is sometimes tempting to just curl up in that corner of mine. I shy away from relationships that infringe upon my privacy. I suppose in some ways I really am enjoying time for myself, but it's hard to strike a balance.

As discussed earlier, friends and family relationships change with divorce, and these changes have a dramatic effect on a person's use of time. Activities that were previously engaged in with certain people may no longer be practical or pleasurable alone. And it takes time to develop new relationships to replace those that are lost. As with the impact of divorce on relationships, the impact on the use of time can also be either positive or negative.

While there is sure to be a period of disorientation until new habits are developed to replace the old ones, this period also offers the possibility of finding new and more satisfying ways to use time. For instance, one woman found a whole new world of activities that brought her a great deal of satisfaction. She learned to ski, to square dance, and began taking all kinds of interesting classes. Even though the divorce had not been of her choosing, she came to feel good about being her own person and thoroughly enjoyed her independence.

BEING SINGLE AGAIN

One of the biggest adjustments to divorce is getting accustomed to the idea of being single again. The longer a person has been married, the more difficult this adjustment is likely to be. Some people find a world they never knew existed, one they can't quite believe.

> *I have made a few ventures out into the "singles" world and it surely is a whole new experience! I can't believe the number of married men who walk around with wedding rings on and still approach whoever might interest them as a partner for the night.*

We can learn a lot about the influence of societal factors on a person's thinking and behavior by following the course of this woman's experience with being single again. She celebrated her fiftieth birthday during the year following her divorce and felt a lot of frustration at her current life situation without a partner. But during the entire first year she found no "suitable, unattached" men, and she began to feel the sexual frustration of being alone.

> *What does a woman do about the problem of being alone? Many things can fill up the time, such as work, but there is still that very real need for sex. I can't accept that that part of my life is over, so*

I've slept with guys that I would never consider "loving." I haven't become promiscuous, but I've spent almost two years without a man and there are still long stretches in between. It does become a problem.

I'm not involved in an ongoing relationship, but I've slept with a married man. I'd never been with any man other than my husband, so I was very curious. I found it to be very exciting and ego-boosting; but for the record, the sex was not as good as with my husband.

By my own "old" standards, the admission I've just made should make me feel I was heading straight for hell, but I don't even feel guilty. I've become much more tolerant of other people's behavior and I do try very hard to not "judge" other people anymore.

This is a very personal view of the thinking of a person in a situation they never expected to become involved in. It provides insight into the dynamics that play a part in the changes in people's attitudes and the accompanying changes in their behavior. When people are in the midst of dealing with a spouse having an affair, they often can't imagine themselves being the "other man" or the "other woman." But as the above experience demonstrates, being alone and trying to start over can cause dramatic changes in a person's thinking.

It's not just women who have difficulty moving into the singles world. According to most studies, men tend to get involved again more quickly than women (and to remarry sooner than women), but being single can be a traumatic experience for them if they're not really free from the effects of what happened in the marriage.

One man was so preoccupied with feelings of rejection due to his ex-wife's affair that he found he was impotent with other women. He finally dealt with this in a most unusual way, by dating his ex-wife's *identical twin* sister. In his mind, she served as a substitute for the wife who had rejected him; so by developing a relationship with the sister (including a sexual relationship), he was able to overcome his feelings of rejection—and his impotence. The motive of the sister was not clear, but the experience allowed him to recover his sense of self-worth so that he could let go of this relationship and go on with his life.

LEARNING TO LOVE AGAIN
· · · · · · ·

Sometimes unresolved issues related to affairs in an earlier marriage present problems in a new relationship. People often have difficulty developing trust in a new partner, even when trust is warranted. For instance, one woman told of her fear that her husband was having an affair, but when she finally began talking about her fears, she learned they were unfounded. However, both of them had been afraid of this happening, as each had been in a previous marriage that ended in divorce because of an affair by their spouse.

Another example of this kind of problem was illustrated in the television sitcom "Cheers." The oft-married Carla was adamant about her belief that her husband was having an affair. He denied it, but she didn't believe him. He reassured her, but she wasn't convinced. Finally, she discovered he really *wasn't* having an affair, and her explanation as to why she hadn't believed him earlier was: "I was never married to anybody who was faithful before."

While it's possible for past experience with affairs to cause unexpected problems in a new relationship, it's also possible to use past experiences to work on a new relationship in a very different way. Some people reach a good understanding of what has happened and take their new understandings into their future relationships. Here's an example of how the issue of monogamy was addressed in a new relationship (which eventually turned into marriage).

> *I am involved in a very satisfying relationship. Monogamy was never an issue we avoided or felt threatened by. We talk about it, but our respect and caring for each other makes us feel that sex with anyone else would not really make sense nor would it feel very comfortable. This is not to say the issue will never arise, only that should it come up, the strength of the bond we now have will see us through.*

Achieving this kind of relationship depends on making good use of what has been learned in going through the difficult process of dealing with a spouse's affair. Hopefully, a person has learned that having a good relationship involves:

- being willing to be honest about everything relevant to the relationship, including attractions to others and how to deal with them.
- being realistic about the difficulties faced by every couple and being willing to work on issues as they arise instead of letting them build up into major grievances.
- acknowledging that people change and being committed to ongoing discussions about thoughts and feelings in all important areas of life (allowing them to know each other as they change).
- functioning in the roles of husband and wife without becoming those roles and losing a sense of individuality.

THE BEST OF BOTH WORLDS

Whether a person decides to stay married or chooses to enter the singles world, they are likely to eventually feel frustrated by the restrictions of their particular choice. Part of the problem that perpetuates affairs is people's desire for the best of both worlds (the best parts of being married and the best parts of being single). They don't want to be trapped in one or the other. Since there are tradeoffs no matter which decision is made, it's important to be clear about the advantages and drawbacks involved in each choice.

For instance, when a person decides to get married, they usually enjoy the sense of togetherness that's involved, but at some point the marriage begins to feel restrictive and they long for more independence and control over their life. If they get a divorce, they may enjoy their newfound freedom until this separateness starts to feel lonely and they begin to miss a sense of togetherness. If they remarry, they're likely to start the cycle all over again.

This is what's happening to many of us who find ourselves caught up in a pattern of marrying, divorcing, remarrying, etc. We're continually trying to satisfy both our need to be connected and our need to be separate. Most of us go through life doing a balancing act between these two needs. When we don't have something, we tend to see only the positive aspects. It's usually not until we get it that we focus on the drawbacks.

One way to increase the chances of staying satisfied with your particular decision over the long haul is to make a deliberate effort to avoid some of the potential drawbacks to your choice by including some of the positive aspects of the *other* choice. This may be the only way to address the issue of "serial monogamy" that results from a succession of marriages.

REDEFINING A *GOOD* MARRIAGE

We've been far too rigid and limited in our way of viewing marriage and what's involved in having a *good* marriage. "Togetherness," for instance, has been greatly overrated as beneficial to a relationship. It may make a nice picture to present to the outside world, but it's often smothering to the two people themselves. The lack of individual involvement in the world probably does more to undermine the overall satisfaction of marriage than any other feature. This is especially true of traditional marriages. By *traditional* I don't necessarily mean "old-fashioned." I just mean the regular marriage situation where the two people are together day in and day out, year in and year out.

The lucky marriages (even when the people involved don't realize it) are those where some outside circumstances dictate a break in this constant togetherness. We see this with many couples who have the money to afford more than one home. They don't always have to be at the same place at the same time, which gives them an opportunity to be apart without either of them "leaving home." But this option is not open to most of us.

If there's no obvious way to accomplish some separate time and space, it creates a significant problem for most people. It's a problem not only because of those around them who are critical of any deliberate separations, but there's usually an uneasy feeling within the couple themselves about arbitrarily seeking time apart.

Job requirements, especially jobs involving travel, often provide a natural means of achieving separate time and space. But I've seen the look of surprise on the faces of people who have heard me acknowledge the positive benefit this has been to my own marriage. The fact that James and I are often separated due to job responsibilities allows us to thoroughly enjoy and relish our time together. I'm convinced that our relationship would not be nearly so exciting and satisfying if we had no opportunity to be alone.

The alone time allows for real solace that enriches my spiritual life in addition to the practical benefits of getting things done alone that are more difficult when we're together. And the time apart certainly brings a different degree of appreciation of our time together.

Of course, there needs to be a fit between the two people involved. If one wants significantly more time apart than the other, this could cause other problems. There also needs to be a high level of honesty and trust in order to prevent the distraction of wondering and worrying about what the other person is doing when they're on their own.

The balance of time together and time apart allows each person to benefit from having a strong connection with another person while still maintaining their own individuality. In this way each person can simultaneously experience some of the benefits of being single along with the benefits of being married, which gives them a better chance of maintaining a satisfying long-term marriage and avoiding the marriage/divorce merry-go-round.

This discussion of the pros and cons of being married and of being single has a direct bearing on the issue of extramarital affairs. Sex per se is only one of the factors involved in having affairs. Much of the appeal of an affair is the sense of being an interesting, attractive person functioning in an independent way. If we have more opportunity to express these aspects of ourselves within marriage, we'll be less likely to feel either a need to get out of the marriage or a need to have an affair as an outlet for our individuality.

11
· · · · · · ·

A New Understanding
of Affairs

How can a person recover after the Monogamy Myth has been shattered? How do they overcome their bitterness or resentment about facing reality? Recovering from any difficult life experience involves using the perspective that can be gained from it to consider other possibilities for achieving personal satisfaction. Many people who have been through the ordeal of dealing with a mate's affair have not only survived, but grown stronger and more secure as a result of their experience.

One particularly inspiring example is the story of one of this country's most famous women. At age thirty-five, Eleanor Roosevelt wrote about her hard-won perspective on life after a period of extreme turmoil: "Somewhere along the line of development we discover what we really are, and then we make our real decision for which we are responsible. Make that decision primarily for yourself because you can never really live anyone else's life, not even your own child's."[1]

While this was the extent of her public statement, the motivation behind it was her recovery from the devastation of learning that her husband was having an affair with one of her most trusted friends. Her private world of safety and security had been destroyed, but she found the inner strength to overcome her shyness and lay claim to a life of her own in becoming one of the world's most remarkable women.

Many people still long for "the good old days" and want to return to a time when things were different, or at least they *thought* they were different. The vision people have in mind is of a couple married for life, living in a house with a picket fence, with two children and a dog named Spot. Regardless of the fact that this image was always more fantasy than reality, these people continually ask the question, "Whatever happened to . . . (monogamy, or being faithful, or abiding by the marriage vows)."

While the nostalgia for a time when things *seemed* to be better is understandable, it's not a useful contribution to dealing with the world as it now exists. Many things are different, including how long people live. A lifelong monogamous marriage when the life expectancy was forty or fifty is very different from a lifelong monogamous marriage when the life expectancy has increased so dramatically. Many people who are studying the ways in which marriage has changed (and is changing) recognize that this is only one of the many changes that affect our chances for monogamy.

Another change is the way women view their role within marriage. Their sense of fairness and desire for independence means they are less likely to stay in marriages that don't satisfy their needs than were women in the past with fewer opportunities and alternatives. And women's changing attitudes are also bringing an increase in the number of women having affairs, so that the old stereotype of affairs as being a primarily male activity is no longer true.

Monogamy may also be affected by the way marriages are lasting a shorter period of time and people are having more marriages during a lifetime. Ironically, there may be more monogamy during some of the shorter marriages due to the fact that people can manage to remain monogamous for this shorter time. One extreme example of this kind of monogamy was illustrated by a man who appeared on a "Donahue" program with his seventeenth wife. In response to the inevitable criticism from the audience about being married so many times, he defended himself by saying he'd never had sex with a woman he wasn't married to. Clearly, this is not what most people think of when they state their belief in monogamy.

Recent reports saying that monogamy is now "in" would seem to reflect a new morality, but they invariably go on to describe how it's people's desire for monogamy that has increased, not their actions. While many people hope for a reduction in the number of extramarital affairs, there is no indication that this will happen. There is no current data to indicate that affairs are declining, despite AIDS or other changes in society. This observation is reflected by a number of recent reports, including that of Annette Lawson in *Adultery:* "Among heterosexual people, there is little sign of change in sexual behavior, especially among the married. If this is so, there will be no less adultery in the near future."[2]

It's hard not to be cynical about monogamy under these circumstances, but an awareness of the current decline of monogamy should not cause us to resign ourselves to the dire predictions for the future. Instead, it should alert us to the need to change our social environment and our assumptions about monogamy that have worked against having a monogamous relationship. My clear personal preference is still for monogamy, and I believe it is possible if we pursue it with more honesty and openness.

Rejecting the Monogamy Myth offers significant benefits, both for individuals and for society as a whole. For the individual, it can bring relief from feelings of personal shame and can bring a realistic assessment of the problem, leading to more honesty and a better chance for developing a monogamous relationship. And for all of us, there's the benefit of no longer living in a society that sabotages the values it espouses by its hypocrisy and secrecy about monogamy and affairs.

OLD ASSUMPTIONS AND NEW UNDERSTANDINGS
• • • • • • •

It's not enough to simply reject the Monogamy Myth. In order to improve the chances for monogamy in our society, it's essential that we replace the old assumptions with new understandings. These can serve both as a prevention of affairs and as a source of recovery when they happen. Following is a list of the old assumptions and new understandings about the most basic aspects of affairs.

THE REASON FOR AFFAIRS

Old: Affairs develop strictly because of the shortcomings and failures of individual men and women. This is a purely personal issue.

New: There are many societal factors that support and contribute to affairs. This is not strictly a personal issue, but a societal issue as well.

SECRECY

Old: Secrecy is the appropriate way to deal with the issue of affairs (since it's strictly a personal matter). This problem should not be openly discussed, but should be handled as quietly as possible.

New: The high degree of secrecy about affairs makes them more likely to happen and makes their impact more difficult to overcome. It's important that this issue be dealt with more openly and more responsibly by society as a whole.

THE PERSON WHO HAS AN AFFAIR

Old: The person who has an affair is weak, insecure, uncaring, or a generally bad person who deserves to be punished.

New: All kinds of people have affairs, not just certain types. Just about any person in this society is vulnerable to having an affair.

THE SPOUSE

Old: The spouse is clearly a victim and deserves either pity for being so mistreated or criticism for failing to keep their mate satisfied.

New: An affair is not a personal reflection on the spouse as a husband or a wife; they are not to blame for their mate's affair.

THE THIRD PARTY

Old: The third party is a special breed of heartless human being. They are selfish and willing to hurt anyone in order to satisfy their own desires.

New: There's a wide variety of people who have affairs with a person who is married, and they have them for a wide variety of reasons. They also usually wind up getting hurt.

TELLING OTHERS

Old: This is such a personal embarrassment that it should not be discussed with other people. It should even be kept hidden from the immediate family if at all possible.

New: Since this isn't a personal failure, pride should not get in the way of talking about this issue. It could happen to anyone personally or to anyone's friends or family.

MARRIAGE VS. DIVORCE

Old: This decision is the first order of business, and it's clear which decision is the "right" one. (Some, of course, think staying married is the right choice, while others think divorce is the only decision.)

New: A decision as critical and complicated as this shouldn't be made in haste. It requires more understanding of the situation in order to make a rational decision rather than an emotional one.

BREAKING THE CODE OF SECRECY
· · · · · · ·

The Monogamy Myth has thrived because of the secrecy surrounding affairs. As long as we don't talk honestly about the reality of what's happening, people will continue to pretend that monogamy is the norm and that society supports monogamy. And as long as this belief persists, people will continue to suffer alone with their sense of failure and shame.

TALKING PERSONALLY

The first step in breaking the code of secrecy about affairs is talking personally about your own experience. The habit of hiding this fact from others serves to reinforce the feelings of shame and embarrassment. Typically, there's been a greater shame felt by men, who seldom admit this experience to anyone. This is reflected by how few men have openly acknowledged that their spouse has had an affair, even if they've gotten a divorce.

Women, too, have traditionally suffered in silence when their partners have had affairs. Their assumption that it reflected on their inadequacies as a woman kept them from talking openly about this experience. Even if they got a divorce, they didn't openly acknowledge this as the cause (except to their closest friends). And if they stayed in the marriage, they quite possibly never told *anyone.*

However, women have gradually begun to openly acknowledge dealing with this issue in their own lives, including some who have written books about their experience. Cynthia Garvey wrote a book describing her experience in surviving the disintegration of her marriage to baseball legend Steve Garvey, who had been involved with another woman for years. As mentioned earlier, Patricia Neal spoke publicly about losing her husband to another woman and included a detailed account of the experience in her book, *As I Am.* And Nora Ephron wrote *Heartburn,* a thinly disguised novel about her own marital breakup because of her husband's affair.

There are several important messages being sent when you speak out about your own experience. You are rejecting the idea that the affair was caused by a personal inadequacy. (And, if you're still *married,* it shows you also understand it was not strictly a personal failure of your spouse.) This causes others to rethink their own attitudes. People expect you to feel embarrassed and ashamed; when you don't, it causes them to stop and wonder why.

Another important benefit of being open about your own experience is that it diminishes the sense of aloneness felt by those people who are still suffering silently, thinking an affair is only their personal problem. For instance, at the time we wrote *Beyond Affairs,* our daughter was a senior in high school. Her best friend asked the English teacher for permission to use our book as the subject of a book report. The teacher agreed—and read the book as well.

A few days later the teacher appeared at my door to tell me that she had known for some time that her husband was having an affair, but had not been able to talk to anyone about it. She knew her relationship was unrecoverable, but she hadn't been able to bring herself to take action. Learning about my experience helped her break her silence and begin to face her own situation.

Within a few months she filed for divorce and began the gradual process of recovering her self-esteem and facing the challenges of being a single mother. She's a bright, talented woman who unnecessarily endured the pain and uncertainty of her situation far longer than necessary, primarily because of the way secrecy has been seen as appropriate in dealing with affairs. Sometimes, all a person needs is to know they're not alone in order to break the code of silence for themselves. And all of us can participate in making this possible.

PUBLIC EXPOSURE

Personal disclosure of information that is relevant to your own life is quite different from spreading rumors or gossip about others. The exposure of individuals against their will is not what I'm advocating by promoting that we break the code of secrecy about this issue. When it comes to telling, it's a matter of "who owns the information."

There was a time when it could be safely assumed that the media would not report information they might have about a person's private life, specifically not exposing any indiscretions. That, however, has changed; they have gone further and further in reporting on the private lives of public people, especially politicians. But before we jump on the media for their part in this situation, we need to recognize that the number of news stories about well-known people involved in affairs is a direct reflection of the public's general fascination with this subject.

One significant trend in recent years has been the number of former third parties who have stepped forward to "tell all" about their involvement with some famous figure from the world of entertainment, sports, or politics. This is certainly shaking up the sense of security many people had felt about their behavior not being exposed. But the one being exposed usually has an interesting reaction; they often put the blame for the consequences of the situation on the third party for talking (as if their own behavior had nothing to do with it). Their attitude seems to be that the real fault is in failing to maintain the secrecy, not in failing to be monogamous in the first place.

IF SOMEONE YOU KNOW IS HAVING AN AFFAIR
· · · · · · ·

If you are considering whether or not you should discuss their behavior with someone you know who is having an affair, the first step is to be honest with yourself about your motives. You should be guided by the closeness of the relationship and your concern for the impact on *their* lives. There are several conditions that should be met before deciding to raise the issue with someone.

- Do you have a very close relationship where they know you really care about them?
- Are you able to avoid seeing them as a bad person for their actions, but understand that there are many factors that brought them to this position?
- Are you concerned about what's best for *them*, not just concerned that they meet your standards of behavior?

If these conditions exist in your relationship and these are your motives for initiating a discussion, then it's likely to be received in the spirit in which it's offered. Any other situation will probably result in resentment for your interference in something they see as none of your business. In other words, any effort to discuss this matter should neither be self-serving nor self-righteous. The effectiveness of anything that is said will be determined by the attitude with which it's approached.

WHAT IF YOU ARE EXPECTED TO COOPERATE IN THE DECEPTION?

Men who are having affairs automatically cooperate with other men in their mutual protection from being discovered. Even if a man is not personally involved in an affair, he will almost always cooperate in the deception in that he will not say or do anything that would be perceived as critical of the men having affairs. He is also likely to feel quite comfortable with supporting the deception if his active cooperation is needed. This general attitude is primarily the result of the male conditioning about how to deal with issues related to sex.

Women are not as likely to be expected to actively cooperate in the deception (except in job situations as described below), but they're expected to cooperate by not deliberately exposing an affair. This difference is partly due to their conditioning, since women are still expected to hold higher sexual standards than men in this society. Women may feel judgmental of someone who is having an affair, but they may still cooperate in the deception; it's just that their motives are different. They may cooperate in keeping an affair hidden for the sake of "protecting" the spouse from the pain of finding out rather than protecting the one having the affair.

While some people have no problem with these situations, others experience ambivalence and frustration at being expected to cooperate in this deception, especially if they see no reasonable way to avoid it. One of the most prevalent instances of this dilemma is when people are expected to cover for coworkers. For instance, secretaries invariably know a lot about the private lives of those for whom they work, and they are routinely called upon to help protect an affair. This can vary from a simple task like accepting collect phone calls from the third party (and always putting them through immediately) to altering expense reports that might expose the presence of the other person.

People are often concerned that their job depends on doing as they are expected, and this is a realistic concern. So it's up to each individual to assess the situation for themselves to determine their degree of discomfort and to weigh these feelings against the practical concerns related to their career.

Another common situation is traveling with a spouse as part of a group where others in the group are not with their mates. Since this degree of openness has been far more prevalent among married men having affairs than among married women having affairs, the problem of cooperating in this deception is usually that of a wife who is on a trip with her husband (usually for a convention or some other kind of business trip). A wife in this situation realizes that she risks her husband's anger (as well as potentially jeopardizing his position with his colleagues) if she doesn't accept the situation and interact with the rest of the group in a perfectly normal way (as if every couple were a married couple and no affairs were taking place).

For those people who feel uncomfortable in these situations, there's no simple solution; each person must make their own decision about how to react. I've personally experienced both of these dilemmas (in the workplace and in work-related travel with my husband), and I cooperated in the sense that I tried as much as possible to ignore what was happening. But we need to face the reality of the prevalence of these situations and make a conscious decision as to how we plan to handle them. Being alert to the possibility of such circumstances makes it possible to avoid some of them. And when they can't be avoided, we need to be honest with ourselves in acknowledging that this is one of the many subtle ways we all cooperate in sustaining the code of secrecy.

DO YOU EVER TELL THE SPOUSE?

There's a special challenge in appropriately handling the situation when the partner of a friend or relative is involved in an affair that has not yet been confronted. It can be very disturbing to be in this position. Naturally, each person will need to assess the situation for themselves, based on their knowledge of the people involved. If it's someone in the immediate family, it's even more a matter for individual determination.

There are some guidelines, however, that can help in dealing responsibly with this issue if it's a friend's partner who is having an affair. (These guidelines may also be helpful in deciding how to deal with the more difficult situation of an affair in the immediate family.) First, if the one having an affair doesn't know that you know, it's probably a good idea to inform them. This may have an effect on their thinking or their behavior, but the purpose is not to threaten or demand; it's simply to make them aware of your knowledge of the affair.

As far as whether or not you should share this information with your friend, it depends on your assessment of whether or not they would want to be told. I know from my own experience that sometimes a person doesn't want to know, and it's not fair to force them to face it at a time they may be unable to deal with it. It's important to know that someone *wants* the information before you give it to them. In other words, if your friend *asks* if you think their partner is having an affair, you probably shouldn't lie. By asking, they are showing a readiness (or at least a willingness) to face it.

However, if they *don't* ask, you should wait for some indication that they either suspect, want to know, or would be able to handle it. So the general rule might be "don't lie, but don't volunteer." In other words, if they ask, they're probably prepared to face it, so you shouldn't lie to them. But if they don't ask, it may be because they really don't want to deal with it yet, so you shouldn't volunteer the information. The best approach would be to help them become better prepared, so that when they finally do confront it, they'll be able to deal with it in a way that allows them to survive the experience.

Of course, there are exceptions. Perhaps you have a joint commitment with a friend or relative to share absolutely everything, and they've made it clear they want you to tell them anything you know that might affect them. If you feel you'd be being dishonest to this commitment by not telling them, then you might not wait for them to ask. As mentioned earlier, this is a very personal decision that each person must make as responsibly as possible for the sake of everyone concerned.

PREVENTING AFFAIRS
· · · · · ·

If you have already faced this issue personally, you're in essence starting over on a whole new phase of life. In order to gain the most possible benefit from your experience, you'll need to accept that you are now different because of this experience—but recognize that you're

OK. You'll also need to see that while no one would choose this as a method of personal growth; nevertheless, that can be the result. It helps to remember: "that which doesn't kill you makes you stronger." There are many ways in which you will be affected by this transformation, but in general you are likely to redefine the way you see yourself and your place in the world. By recovering from this experience, you are prepared to face the future without repeating the false ways of thinking about preventing affairs that you may have blindly accepted before. Whether with the same partner or another, you now have a chance to think clearly about what's at stake and what's involved in having a monogamous relationship. Reading the following guidelines can reinforce what you've already learned the hard way. And for those of you who have not personally faced this crisis, these are critical understandings if you are to prevent affairs.

What is most likely to prevent affairs:

Being aware that no one is immune from having an affair, discussing and agreeing on a commitment to monogamy, regularly renewing your commitment, engaging in on-going, honest communication about everything that impacts your relationship, and acknowledging that the issue of monogamy is never settled once and for all.

What will NOT prevent affairs:

Being "in love," promising to be faithful, threats or ultimatums, religious commandments or parental injunctions, having more children, getting caught, repeating the marriage vows, spicing up your sex life, trying to be "perfect," and trying to meet all your partner's needs.

PREVENTION DEPENDS ON KNOWING "WHY"

If you want to prevent affairs, you need a clear understanding of why affairs happen in the first place. Most of us tend to think that a partner's affair has to be due to some failure on our part to meet their needs. Unfortunately, by thinking an affair is due to unmet needs, we set ourselves up to take the blame when our partner has an affair—and to take the responsibility for keeping it from happening. While the desire to meet each other's needs is an important feature of a good relationship, this effort (by both parties) will spring freely from love—not from fear that a failure to do so will *cause* our partner to have an affair. So while unmet needs may be a quick and easy *excuse*, it's not the reason people have affairs.

There's never just one simple reason; there are *many* reasons. Usually it's a combination of three different kinds of forces that are working together: forces that PUSH people toward affairs, forces that PULL people toward affairs, and the societal factors. (As you can see below, unmet needs are included in the group of factors that *push* people toward affairs.)

1. Forces that *push* people toward affairs:

Desire to escape or find relief from a painful relationship; Boredom; Desire to fill gaps in an existing relationship; Desire to punish one's partner; Need to prove one's attractiveness or worth; Desire for more attention or other unmet needs.

2. Forces that *pull* people toward affairs:

Attraction (sex, companionship, admiration); Power; Novelty; Excitement, risk, or challenge; Curiosity; Enhanced self-image; "Falling in love."

3. Societal influences:

I won't repeat the societal factors here—because I have discussed them throughout the book. While the powerful influence of social factors has largely been ignored, they are at the heart of the ability to recover from a partner's affair. As long as affairs are seen *only* in terms of personal failure and personal blame, it's difficult to overcome the feelings of pain, anger, resentment, bitterness, or guilt. Calling attention to these social factors does not excuse individual responsibility; it simply serves to bring some balance to our understanding of why affairs happen and how to avoid them.

ONLINE AFFAIRS

• • • • • •

The Internet is exploding with opportunities for developing "Online Affairs"—and we're only beginning to see the fall-out from this new arena for people to engage in affairs. Dealing with the impact of the World Wide Web will be one of the most challenging areas as far as preventing affairs in the future. Although not initially involving physical contact, Online Affairs are highly-charged, sexually. They involve the same kinds of thinking and emotions as other affairs (including the secrecy, fantasy, and excitement, as well as the denial and rationalization) and they have the same potential for being devastating to the primary relationship.

Here's a typical scenario:

1. You spend more and more time Online.

   Online interactions provide an escape from the realities of day-to-day living. The fantasy world online can make the real world seem dull and boring. The sheer numbers of people create unlimited potential for newness.

2. You meet someone interesting Online.

   You share confidences: hopes, fears, fantasies. The intense sharing brings you closer and closer together. You fantasize about being more than online friends. You become infatuated with your "friend" and want more and more interaction. You feel like you're "in love."

3. Your primary partner suspects/knows about your online friend.

   You deny or rationalize about your online activity. Your partner becomes increasingly suspicious and feels more and more anxious. You ignore or deny the impact this is having on your partner. Your partner learns more details and is devastated by the situation. You tell yourself that since there's no actual sex involved, it shouldn't matter. You grow closer to your online friend and more distant from your partner.

4. You want to meet your online friend in person.

   You feel like "soul-mates" or that you were meant for each other. You consider risking it all to see your online friend. You either meet and engage in sex or you don't and feel like star-crossed lovers.

5. Your life has been changed in ways you never intended.

   Your online relationship ends—and your primary relationship may end as well.

Reflections on this scenario:

The above scenario is so common as to allow for some general observations. First, any new connection is going to be exciting, but it may not be the particular person who makes the difference. The excitement has more to do with the nature of the relationship than to the feelings about a specific person. In any new relationship (whether or not it begins online), people present the best sides of themselves; it's not reflective of the whole person functioning in the real world.

Whatever loss you feel when the Online Affair ends is the loss of a fantasy, not the real thing. All too often we think of love only as the initial heady feelings of love. Falling in love (or new love) produces some of the most intense feelings you will ever experience, but it doesn't last. While it may be a fantastic experience, much of the intensity of the feeling is inherent in its newness and novelty. Once a "fantasy" love takes on all the real-life responsibilities of a long-term relationship, the feelings either make the transition into the next, deeper stage of love, or they wither. So comparing the feelings in a new relationship with the feelings of a long-term marriage is like comparing apples and oranges.

As for the impact on the primary relationship, it's common to rationalize an online affair as being OK because it's "not really an affair." But it often has the potential for being as devastating to the partner as a sexual affair. (In fact, most people whose partners have a sexual affair find that they recover from the fact that their partner had sex with someone else before they recover from the fact that they were deceived.)

We like to think that deception is only involved with outright lying. But a more accurate definition of a lack of honesty in a relationship is "withholding relevant information." Anything that is deliberately hidden from a partner (whether it's the fact of being involved in an online affair or the specifics of the online interactions) creates an emotional distance that presents a serious problem that is difficult to overcome.

So while people may disagree about the definition of an affair, there's no mistaking the impact of Online Affairs on the partner who is feeling fearful and hurt. When these feelings are ignored or dismissed as unreasonable, it shows a lack of caring that may be more of a threat to the relationship than the affairs themselves.

Online Affairs often lead to diminishing or destroying the primary relationship—although this was not the original intention. And in hindsight, many people who wind up having affairs recognize that they could have/should have known what they were getting into, but they simply blocked it out. A common lament is, "I didn't intend to have an affair."

When it comes to Online Affairs, it's not just a question of whether it's wrong, but also whether it's smart. In looking for something better in life or a way to get more out of life, people often wind up with less. It's important to find some other avenue for igniting the positive, fully alive feelings that are a big part of the enticement of Online Affairs. Their appeal can serve as a signal to rethink all aspects of life and determine what can be done to feel more "alive" that is rooted in reality (instead of fantasy)—and that does not come with such a high price.

FUTURE GENERATIONS
• • • • • • •

Dealing with affairs after they happen is only one aspect of addressing this issue more responsibly. We can make a significant difference in the *prevention* of affairs if we begin raising kids who don't learn that sexual desire and deception go hand in hand. This means being more willing to realistically face the sexual realities of teenagers today by making it possible for them to talk to us about sexual issues. This need will grow ever more critical with the expanding influence of the Internet—which will expose future generations to more sexually-oriented material than TV or movies ever did. They will use the Internet like we currently use the telephone, and no efforts at censorship or "protection" can address the problems they will face as a result.

Our hope for influencing their development into sexually responsible adults lies in our commitment to more honest communication about all aspects of sex, monogamy, relationships, and marriage. Of course, this means "practicing what we preach" by demonstrating within the family the importance of honest communication. Future generations can only learn honesty by seeing it in their own families. So by helping our own relationships become more honest, we provide the kind of training that makes it more likely that our children will have relationships based on a commitment to honesty. This increase in the level of honesty between couples can greatly enhance the satisfaction that's possible in a loving relationship, as well as reduce the likelihood of extramarital affairs.

As a society, we need to acknowledge our role in perpetuating affairs and take more responsibility for dealing with the societal factors that support them. We also need to adopt a more compassionate attitude toward the people whose lives are affected by affairs. It's hard enough on those personally dealing with this issue without compounding their pain by our harsh way of judging them.

It is my hope that more understanding and perspective can bring recovery to those individuals who face it personally and bring change to us as a society of people who care about making things better, both for today and for the generations to come.

• • • • • • •

Notes

CHAPTER 1
1. Carol Botwin. "Advice." *New Woman,* October 1988.
2. David Viscott. *I Love You, Let's Work It Out.* New York: Simon & Schuster, 1987.
3. Alexandra Penney. *How to Make Love to Each Other.* New York: Berkley, 1984.
4. Melvyn Kinder and Connell Cowan. *Husbands and Wives.* New York: Clarkson N. Potter, 1989.
5. Mary Ann Bartusis. *Every Other Man.* New York: E. P. Dutton, 1978.
6. Philip Blumstein and Pepper Schwartz. *American Couples.* New York: William Morrow, 1983.
7. Annette Lawson. *Adultery.* New York: Basic Books, 1988.
8. Lynn Atwater. *The Extramarital Connection.* New York: Irvington, 1982.
9. Frank Pittman. *Private Lies.* New York: W. W. Norton, 1989.
10. Jessie Bernard. *The Future of Marriage.* New York: World, 1972.

CHAPTER 2
1. Herb Goldberg. *The New Male Female Relationship.* New York: William Morrow, 1983.
2. Ibid.
3. Melvyn Kinder and Connell Cowan. *Husbands and Wives.* New York: Clarkson N. Potter, 1989.
4. John Powell. *The Secret of Staying in Love.* Niles, Ill.: Argus, 1974.
5. Joseph and Lois Bird. *Marriage Is for Grownups.* New York: Doubleday, 1969.
6. Carol Botwin. "Advice." *New Woman,* October 1988.

CHAPTER 3
1. James and Peggy Vaughan. *Beyond Affairs*. Hilton Head, S.C.: Dialog Press, 1980.
2. Ibid.

CHAPTER 4
1. Allen Wheelis. *On Not Knowing How to Live*. New York: Harper & Row, 1975.
2. Ibid.

CHAPTER 7
1. Lewis Yablonsky. *The Extra-Sex Factor*. New York: Times Books, 1979.
2. Warren Farrell. *Why Men Are the Way They Are*. New York: McGraw-Hill, 1986.
3. Peter Kreitler. *Affair Prevention*. New York: Macmillan, 1981.

CHAPTER 8
1. James and Peggy Vaughan. *Beyond Affairs*. Hilton Head, S.C.: Dialog Press, 1980.

CHAPTER 9
1. Melba Colgrove, Harold Bloomfield, and Peter McWilliams. *How to Survive the Loss of a Love*. New York: Lion Press, 1976.
2. Judith Wallerstein and Sandra Blakeslee. *Second Chances*. New York: Ticknor & Fields, 1989.
3. Ibid.

CHAPTER 10
1. Patricia Neal. *As I Am*. New York: Simon & Schuster, 1988.

CHAPTER 11
1. Joseph P. Lash. *Eleanor and Franklin*. New York: W. W. Norton, 1971.
2. Annette Lawson. *Adultery*. New York: Basic Books, 1988.

Bibliography

Ahrons, Constance. *The Good Divorce.* New York: HarperCollins, 1994.

Barbach, Lonnie, and Geisinger, David L. *Going the Distance.* New York: NAL/Dutton, 1993.

Bernard, Jessie. *The Future of Marriage.* New Haven, CT: Yale University Press, 1982.

Bok, Sissela. *Lying: Moral Choice in Public and Private Life.* New York: Random House, 1989.

Brownmiller, Susan. *Femininity.* New York: Fawcett Book Group, 1985.

Colgrove, Melba; Bloomfield, Harold; and McWilliams, Peter. *How to Survive the Loss of a Love.* New York: Prelude Press, 1993.

Fisher, Helen E. *Anatomy of Love: The Natural History of Monogamy, Adultery, and Divorce.* New York: Fawcett Book Group, 1994.

Gottman, John. *Why Marriages Succeed or Fail.* New York: Simon & Schuster, Inc. 1995.

Hendricks, Gay and Kathlyn. *Conscious Loving.* New York: Bantam, 1992.

Heyn, Dalma. *The Erotic Silence of the American Wife.* New York: NAL/Dutton, 1993.

Jampolsky, Gerald G., and Cirincione, Diane V. *Love is the Answer.* New York: Bantam, 1991.

Kinder, Melvyn, and Cowan, Connell. *Husbands and Wives.* New York: NAL/Dutton, 1990.

Kirshenbaum, Mira. *Too Good to Leave, Too Bad to Stay.* New York: Penguin Books, 1997.

Kushner, Harold S. *When Bad Things Happen to Good People.* New York: Avon, 1997.

Lawson, Annette. *Adultery.* New York: Basic Books, 1988.

Lerner, Harriet. *The Dance of Deception*. New York: HarperCollins, 1994.

Lerner, Harriet. *The Dance of Intimacy*. New York: HarperCollins, 1990.

Lusterman, Don-David. *Infidelity: A Survival Guide*. Oakland, CA: New Harbinger Publications, 1998.

Marlin, Emily. *Relationships in Recovery*. New York: HarperCollins, 1990.

Pietsch, William. *Human BE-ing*. New York: NAL/Dutton, 1984.

Pittman, Frank. *Private Lies*. New York: W. W. Norton, 1990.

Richardson, Laurel. *The New Other Woman*. New York: The Free Press, 1987.

Rubin, Lillian B. *Intimate Strangers*. New York: HarperCollins, 1990.

Scarf, Maggie. *Intimate Partners*. New York: Ballantine Books, 1988.

Schwartz, Pepper. *Love Between Equals*. New York: The Free Press, 1995.

Spring, Janis Abrahms. *After the Affair*. New York: HarperCollins, 1997.

Subotnik, Rona, and Harris, Gloria. *Surviving Infidelity*. Holbrook, MA: Bob Adams, 1994.

Tannen, Deborah. *You Just Don't Understand*. New York: William Morrow, 1994.

Triere, Lynette, and Peacock, Richard. *Learning to Leave*. New York: Warner Books, 1993.

Vaughan, James and Peggy. *Beyond Affairs*. La Jolla, CA: Dialog Press, 1980.

Vaughan, James and Peggy. *Making Love Stay*. La Jolla, CA: Dialog Press, 1997.

Wallerstein, Judith, and Blakeslee, Sandra. *Second Chances*. New York: Houghton Mifflin Company, 1996.

Weiner-Davis, Michele. *Divorce Busting*. New York: Simon & Schuster, 1993.

Welwood, John. *Journey of the Heart*. New York: HarperCollins, 1996.

Psychology & Self-Help Books from Newmarket Press

Ask for these titles at your local bookstore or send this coupon to:
Newmarket Press, 18 East 48th Street, Suite 1501, New York, NY 10017;
Tel.: 212-832-3575; Fax: 212-832-3629.